Women in Management

Women in Management

Douglas C. Basil

with the collaboration of
Edna Traver
Research Associate

Foreword by Edith Head

DUNELLEN
New York

Contents

2 Incidence of Women in Managerial Positions 19

3 Positive Company Attitudes Toward Women in Management 31

4 Negative Company Attitudes Toward Women in Management 47

List of Tables and Figures

Foreword

The concept of women in management always seems to raise the spectre of a hard-driving and almost totally unfeminine executive. Perhaps the stereotype of the movie versions of the 1930's and 40's still colors the acceptance of women as managers who have failed to retain their femininity. The women's liberation movement has brought to the surface the latent and largely unfulfilled desires of many women to contribute more directly to the professions, the arts, to government and to business. As Professor Basil emphasizes in his book, women constitute the greatest untapped resource in our economy.

As a woman in business, I would like to take this opportunity to share some of my philosophy and my experiences with the reader. Let there be no misunderstanding; education is the greatest prerequisite for success for any woman. In my own case, although I am now a designer for the movie industry and my formal education was not in design, the scholastic preparation that I obtained in the university provided me with the confidence and understanding necessary for my life-long career. Almost equally important as formal education is the readiness women must have to prepare for and accept change. The movie industry is a prime example of how extensive change can be. The monolithic structure of the industry with its major movie studios and stables of stars and starlettes has given way to an almost back lot type of production, often with the streets being used as the background for a movie. Stars have become producers and directors with their own companies and the burgeoning cost of making a movie in Hollywood has led to extensive foreign productions. How can one exist and be successful under such drastically changing conditions?

My experience dictates that the successful woman must be ready for change and not depend upon a platform which she thinks can last forever. Not only have we seen change in technologies and management but also in the very attitude of people to work itself. The woman in management must learn to relate to all her co-workers, her subordinates, and her boss. People now want to work **with** the manager rather than **under** the manager. This requires that the woman in management be tremendously flexible and patient. Management no longer requires the heavy hand of authority but the soft kid glove of persuasion. Today and tomorrow we are dealing with temperament, feelings, and sentiment all the way up and down the managerial ladder.

It is interesting that my work as a designer, unlike the great couturiers who deal with individual creativity, is really working with people, designing for people, and in reality translating human beings into the characters they really are. This requires me to be a part of a team and in effect to integrate myself into the totality of what the director is trying to achieve in his picture and in a particular scene. Really, all managers now are managers of a team, and women have some very special qualities that they can add to such a team, as Dr. Basil's research shows. The woman's job is to harness those qualities, be flexible enough to recognize her changing relationships with others, and contribute to the best of her ability to the team effort.

Edith Head

Universal City, California
May, 1972

Preface

The interest in making this study was generated by the author's involvement in a number of special management development programs for executive women sponsored by the Executive Programs Office of the Graduate School of Business at the University of Southern California. The increasing demands by industry and government for highly qualified managers and the seemingly decreasing supply of talent emphasize the need to tap sources of supply other than the traditional male college graduate. One answer to this need is to utilize women to a much higher degree than at present in managerial positions, including the top management or executive ranks.

One of the major purposes of this study was to determine the specific barriers to the promotion of women into managerial positions. Was the unwillingness to both develop and utilize women managers the result of a deep-seated prejudice by males to females in equal or superior positions, or were there perhaps logical and technical reasons? It is hoped that the partial answers supplied by this research study will generate and spawn additional research to permit a deeper understanding of the apparent prejudice against women in management and provide the means whereby such prejudice can be minimized or eliminated for future generations.

The author would like to take this opportunity to give special thanks to Mrs. Dorothy Ford and the Business and Professional Women's Foundation for its support of the study and for all the help they provided in making the fruits of the research available to the general public.

Douglas C. Basil
Los Angeles, California

1   The Status of Women at Work

Women constitute the greatest untapped source of managerial, professional, and technical talent in the United States. There are few social taboos against women working, as evidenced by the fact that one out of every three workers is a woman and some 60 percent of these working women are married. Yet the proportion of women in managerial positions is extremely low. Utilizing the criterion of income as the measure of the number of women in managerial positions, we find some 13 percent of working women earning over $10,000 per year, compared to fewer than 1 percent of women in this income bracket.[1]

The Role of Women in the Labor Force

Many factors have contributed to the increase in the number of working women:

1. Technological advances creating jobs requiring little physical effort.

2. Development of labor-saving devices and products for the home permitting women to both work and look after a home.

3. Economic growth of the nation creating new job opportunities and labor shortages.

4. Federal legislation creating equal opportunities for women.

5. Rising expectation level requiring incomes from both husband and wife.

Despite the fantastic increase in the number of working women, the majority of women are in lower paying occupations with few women in managerial positions. Even in professions dominated by women, there are comparatively few women in managerial positions. In education, some 70 percent of teachers in the elementary and secondary schools are women and yet only 37 percent of elementary school principals and less than 4 percent of secondary school principals are women.[2]

The Federal Government has passed legislation to grant greater equality and opportunity for women. Title VII of the Civil Rights Act of 1964 prohibited discrimination because of sex in hiring and promoting employees with the act effective for firms with twenty-five or more employees by July 1968.[3] The 1963 Equal Pay Act gave women paycheck equality with men doing like work.[4]

Legislation has not provided the complete remedy for sexual discrimination. The National Organization for Women, formed in 1966 to bring "true equality to all women in America," claims the Civil Rights Act has not been enforced and that women are still the victims of prejudice and discrimination.[5]

There is little doubt that there is discrimination against women in advancing them to managerial positions. The question is to determine what form such discrimination takes and what prescription might be available to end such discrimination. It is the purpose of this study to determine attitudes toward women in management by both men and women.

Purpose of the Study

The University of Southern California, under a grant from the Business and Professional Women's Foundation, undertook a mail questionnaire study of private companies and government agencies to determine attitudes toward women in management. The objectives of the study included the following:

1. To document the personnel practices of diverse industries of various sizes and located in different geographical areas regarding women in managerial positions. Reactions and answers to the following questions were sought by means of the mail questionnaire:

   a. Are there characteristics common to firms in which women have advanced to management positions?

   b. What types of management positions do women hold?

   c. What importance does size of company or nature of business bear to the issue?

   d. Does woman's biological role of wife and mother have a detrimental effect on consideration for promotion of women in their child-bearing years?

e. Does the legislation limiting women's hours of work have a negative effect on their advancement?

f. What factors influence companies toward hiring a woman as a potential manager when she re-enters the labor market after her children are grown? Do women have singular qualifications which are recognized as assets, or are women accepted merely because of external pressures and/or the military obligations of their male counterparts?

g. What reasons are offered by those companies which refuse to hire a woman for management training when she returns to the business world? Do women possess inherent characteristics necessary for management? What factors in their backgrounds make women less adequate than men?

2. To obtain profiles of the male and female respondents in regard to age, academic education, work experience, and family background, and to explore their personal opinions and attitudes toward women in business, particularly in regard to the following broad categories:

a. What are the special skills and characteristics important to various levels of management? Are there differences in perception between the sexes?

b. What personality characteristics and mental abilities are required for top level management? Which sex is more likely to possess them?

c. How do successful male and female executives view women's role on the management team? Do women really want and deserve responsibility? Do subordinates approve of women bosses? How do the women respondents differ from the men in their acceptance of women managers?

Research Methodology

The survey population for the mail questionnaire consisted of approximately 2,000 organizations including companies, local, state, and Federal Government agencies, chosen to provide information from very small to very large organizations in all geographical areas. Included in the company sample were firms from the manufacturing, merchandising, banking, insurance, transportation, and utility industries. Two questionnaires were mailed to each selected company, one to be completed by the highest ranking male executive to whom women managers reported, and the other by the highest ranking female executive. [6]

The first section of the questionnaire was structured to provide factual information regarding the incidence of women in managerial positions, defined as at least one level above forelady, the types of managerial positions held by women, and company policy on the promotion of women. The remaining sections were designed to uncover male and female attitudes toward women in management.

Over 300 responses, including those of 102 female executives and 214 male executives, were received from the mail questionnaire for a total of 16 percent response. The unwillingness of a number of organizations, particularly very large ones, to participate in any questionnaire research, and the potential legal implications in completing the questionnaire may have contributed to the relatively low response. [7]

Table 1 presents the classification of the responses to the mail questionnaire by type of business, size of company, and regional distribution. The breakdown of male responses by industry is shown in Figure 1, and of female responses in Figure 2.

The survey sought to distinguish attitudes and managerial practices by size of firm and geographical location. Table 1 presents the classifications of responses which favor slightly the West and larger organizations.[8]

In addition to the analysis of the mail questionnaire, this report draws upon the literature uncovered in an extensive literature research, upon a series of in-depth interviews with female and male executives, and upon the analysis of 200 questionnaires completed by male and female liberal arts undergraduates. The bibliography indicates the widespread interest in the subject of women at work, particularly since the passage of Title VII of the Civil Rights Act of 1964.

An Overview of the Research Results

The purpose of this section is to provide a summary overview of the results of the research study. The overview presents the conclusions from the research study without the statistical detail which might confuse the reader interested in more general conclusions.

Survey Population

To study the incidence of and attitudes toward women in management, some 2,000 questionnaires were mailed (of which 300 were completed), in-depth interviews were conducted, and 200 questionnaires were completed by undergraduate students. With one out of every three workers a woman, and some 60 percent of working women married, the potential discrimination against women in management is a far more critical issue than many cases of discrimination occupying the national scene.

Table 1

Returns from the Mail Survey of U. S. Industries
by Type of Business and Size of Company

Number of Employees

Type of Business	To 500		501-1000		1001-5000		5001-20,000		20,001-50,000		Over 50,000		None Specified		TOTAL	
	Men	Women	Men	Women	Men	Women	Men	Women	Men	Women	Men	Women	Men	Women	Men	Women
Manufacturing	32	12	17		22	6	25	10	9	4	1	1	1		107	32
Merchandising	5	7	3	1	4	1	5	5			1			1	18	8
Banking	11	7	1		6	3	2	4	1						21	14
Insurance	3						2	2							5	2
Transportation & Utilities	1		1		4		4	1	1	1	1				12	2
Government	3	9	5	3	18	15	10	5	1	2	2	1		2	39	37
Other	2	1	2		3	2	3	2			1				11	5
None Specified													1	2	1	2
TOTAL	57	29	29	4	57	27	51	29	12	7	6	1	2	5	214	102

by Geographical Region

	Men	Women
Northeast	45	21
South	40	20
Central	53	24
West	65	33
Many Regions	7	
None Specified	4	4

7

Figure 1
Breakdown of Male Responses by Industry

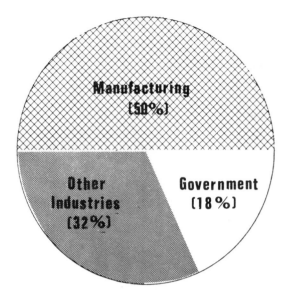

Figure 2
Breakdown of Female Responses by Industry

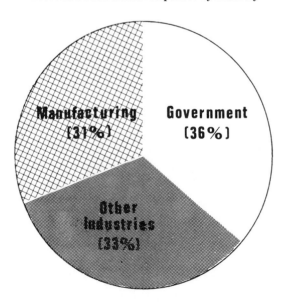

Incidence of Women in Management

The proportion of women in managerial positions was unbelievably small:

1. More than 70 percent of the companies responding had only some 3 percent of managerial positions staffed by women.

2. In staff and professional managerial positions, women tended toward governmental positions with, for example, the percentage of women lawyers in government three times the national average of women lawyers to male lawyers.

3. Women rarely had managerial positions in production or marketing with the exception of merchandising.

4. Women rarely held top managerial positions, with fewer than one firm in four having any women in upper levels of management.

Positive Attitudes Toward Women in Management

Although there were obvious prejudices against women in management, there were also a number of positive attitudes:

Marriage—The possibility that women would leave to marry was not considered a barrier to promotion and hiring.

Legal Limitations on Work—There was little feeling that the existence of any laws limiting the work activities of women precluded them from management positions.

Re-entry of Women After Marriage—There were positive attitudes toward women re-entering the labor market after marriage, with 90 percent of government agencies and over 60 percent of merchandising and banking firms willing to hire women equally with men. The other industries surveyed were far less willing to hire women returning to the labor market.

Equal Pay with Men—The majority of responding firms

indicated that they did not utilize women as managers because of lower pay although the literature cites many instances of women managers complaining about salary discrimination.

Accept Women Only Because of Male Shortage—The predominant attitude was that women would be accepted for management development and training not because of a shortage of males but on the basis of potential for managerial positions.

Acceptance of Women Only Where Men Do Not Compete for Jobs—The competition for managerial jobs was strong in every industry and even for those jobs usually held by women. But there was evidence that young men resented being bossed by married women who "did not have to work."

Women Hired for Stability—It was felt by the majority of respondents that stability was not a major factor and that mobility among executives was not particularly greater for males than for females.

Woman's Point of View—Except for merchandising and banking, the hiring of women for managerial positions strictly to take advantage of the special factor of obtaining a "woman's point of view" was not considered a major reason for hiring women for managerial positions.

Negative Attitudes Toward Women in Management

The majority of negative attitudes were realted in some way to work performance rather than to emotional evaluation of women as belonging in the home and not in the office. But the negative factors weighed heavily with most firms listing more than one reason for the lack of acceptance of women for managerial positions.

Age and Training—Although it was recognized that there was heavy expense involved in management training, there did not seem to be a strong prejudice against women for managerial training positions or against older women in particular. But the proportion of women in any managerial positions would point to the conclusion that women were rarely accepted for such training programs.

Women as Managers—Companies with women in executive positions tended to be more favorable toward the idea that women make good managers. In firms without women in executive positions the attitude was just the opposite, although this was less true in larger firms than in smaller.

Women Have Inadequate Business Experience—Most firms supported the concept that long years away from business or a profession hampered even well qualified women seeking managerial positions. It was felt that a major reason that there were not more women in managerial positions was that they lacked the qualifications for management.

Lack of Geographical Mobility—A large number of firms (with the notable exception of government agencies) were unwilling to consider women for management because it was felt that women could not relocate since the primary career in a family was usually that of the husband.

Women Do Not Have Appropriate Educational Background—The survey indicated that women were considered to have adequate but not exceptional educational backgrounds. This resulted in firms preferring men over women in general because men had more extensive educational backgrounds than women.

Women Lack Drive and Motivation for Management—The results of the survey generally confirmed the belief that women are not career oriented. At least 20 percent of the companies failed to consider women seriously for managerial positions because they felt that women lacked the necessary drive and motivation to be really successful in managerial positions and to stand the pressures and tensions of management. Undoubtedly the balance between the home responsibilities of a marriage and the business responsibilities makes it difficult for women to apply the drive and motivation of their male counterparts. A consequence of this problem of balance was that a high proportion of women who did achieve higher management positions were single or divorced.

Profile of the Respondents

To provide more meaning to the responses and the conclusions drawn in the survey, it is necessary to look at the respondents themselves.

Age Distribution—The only aspect common to men and women respondents was that more than three-fourths were over forty. Almost 90 percent of men were married compared to less than 40 percent of the women. Women in small firms were more likely to be married than in large ones. More than 50 percent of the men had college degrees, compared to one in three women. Of these women, the educational level was interrelated with age. The majority of women with college degrees were younger. There were more degreed women in large firms than in small, which may be due to a greater percentage of the women in small companies being owners or co-owners.

Length of Service as Managers—Women respondents had considerably less experience in management than male respondents. Generally, both men and women managers in smaller firms had greater length of service as managers than those in very large corporations. In the large firms, 70 percent had been managers less than twenty years. Over 80 percent of both men and women respondents had supervised women supervisors. Size had little significance, except that in giant corporations a larger percentage of women respondents had supervised women managers.

Family Background—A small proportion of both parents of respondents had been to college but almost two-thirds of the fathers were either professional men or held management positions. Less than half of the mothers were employed, but three times as many mothers of the women respondents were professional women.

Wife Husband—About three-fourths of the husbands of married women respondents (37 percent married) were college trained compared to barely half of the wives of male respondents (89 percent married). About half of the wives worked and one-third of those had professional positions. The husbands of over 90 percent of women respondents had high ranking positions.

Personal Attitudes Toward Managerial Qualifications

In order to determine if the frame of references of male and female executives differed, the questionnaire asked respondents to note the personal characteristics of top management and whether these were more common to men or women. There were very similar responses by both male and female managers to ranking of characteristics. "Decisiveness," "Consistency and Objectivity," and "Emotional Stability" ranked at the top, although in a different order of response (but with the same relative importance). The remaining characteristics receiving majority response as being important were "Analytical Ability," "Perception and Empathy," "Loyalty," "Interest in People," and "Creativity." Men and women gave the same order of importance to these characteristics. Interestingly, "Attention to Detail" was noted as a required characteristic of top management by 40 percent of all respondents.

Are these characteristics more common to men or women? A large percentage left this question blank with a greater number of blanks than for any other portion of the questionnaire, which suggests uncertainty as to which sex was more analytical, decisive, etc. Of the eight characteristics considered important for management women were said to have four, all of which ranked low on the list. Even the women respondents rated themselves as having only the "Human Relations" characteristics of "Perception and Empathy," "Creativity," "Loyalty," and "Interest in People." The responses of the undergraduate students followed the same pattern as executives. The literature search supports these findings, noting that women were "temperamentally unfit" for management. There was some diversity of opinion in the literature, but generally it was stated that women are not as rational as men, cannot be as objective, are inclined to jealousy and to make decisions based on emotionalism. On the opposite side, most of the articles agree with the results of our survey: that women have flair for people, that they are more likely to be understanding of another's needs, all of which consequently leads to the acceptance of women in personnel, welfare, etc.

Personal Opinions on Career Interests Vs. Personal Interests

The majority rejected the premise that women were less interested in their jobs than men. Since most of the women in the mail survey were single or divorced, it seems logical that these women would feel dedicated to their jobs. The relationship between attitudes and work experiences indicated that men who had worked with women, either as non-management subordinates or management subordinates, were more positive in their attitudes toward women in management. The literature supports the view that working women with grown families are as dependable and conscientious as men.

Most executives, both men and women, agreed that a woman's job interests must be subservient to her husband's, therefore hindering a woman's promotability. In the case of considering single women as potential managers, an overwhelming majority of respondents agreed that a single woman is as content in her job as her male counterpart.

Attitudes Toward Management Training for Women

The majority of both sexes agreed, with male respondents supporting the statement more strongly than female respondents, that a male is a far better candidate for management training than a female. An interesting point was that women in merchandising and banking favored men to a greater extent than the average of women respondents.

An Assessment of Mobility

Although the majority of both sexes indicated that it is too much 'of a gamble to spend thousands of dollars in management training on a woman of child-bearing age, the women respondents said it was just as risky to spend such monies on male candidates. The attitude was that any young man becomes impatient for advancement and finds the quickest road to promotion by changing employers, which conclusions were also reached by other studies.

Preference Toward Utilizing Women in Professional Rather Than Supervisory Assignments

Most respondents supported the argument that women possess certain personality traits which lessen their chances for acceptance as managers. The predominant opinion was that women are best used in staff positions. Women executives in manufacturing were very strong in support of this contention, which reflected the fact that a high proportion of the respondents held professional positions.

Managerial Prejudices Against Women

Men and women both agreed that women are more emotional and less logical than men. The male attitude, denied by female sexes, was that women cannot take the pressures required of an executive.

Men and women both agreed that women, more than men, have a subjective ability to understand the needs and feelings of others. But the men felt that this in itself does not make women better managers of subordinates. The women respondents disagreed with this position.

Men and women agreed that there still is prejudice against women working outside the home and that this attitude is deeply rooted in our culture. There was very strong support by both sexes that men (and even women, to a lesser degree) do not like to work for women, and that women create problems of insecurity in both sexes. Other studies reported similar findings, that men in general find working for a woman rather repulsive. A more favorable attitude was expressed by men who had experience with women as subordinates or as superiors. The vast majority of both sexes agreed there is bias against women which prevents full utilization of their talents. There was a high degree of negativism among students, with both male and female students expressing the opinion that males feel inferior when working for a woman.

Women in Management Unacceptable as Peers

The survey found that differences in sexes caused significant problems in working relationships. These views were supported both by men and (to a lesser degree) by women. In merchandising, 100 percent of the female executives who responded to the questions reported that women were not accepted as equal, and in the other industries the survey found decided masculine resentment against women in management ranks.

Greater antipathy toward women in management was

shown by male students, who could be considered the future generation of businessmen, than by male executives. This suggests that the prejudices against women in management will not diminish in the so-called permissive generation. The attitude does not offer much hope for the future status of women in management.

Women as a Managerial Resource

There is a critical shortage of trained personnel, and industry is faced with the necessity of considering women as a management resource. Women, as well as men, are attaining higher educational levels. The predictions are that by 1980 thirty-two million women will be employed, or one and one-half times as many as in 1960. Most executives agree there are prejudices against women in management, but feel women are at least partially responsible for perpetuating the prejudices. Legislation has been of some value in enhancing the status of women, but whether women succeed in their goal of equality with men depends to a considerable extent on their individual values and their willingness to dedicate themselves to careers with managerial responsibilities. The opportunities appear to be at hand and the boundaries which divide men's work from women's work have been somewhat overcome, but the woman aspiring to management who is as well qualified as her male counterpart, or even better qualified, is faced with discrimination simply because of her sex.

The following chapters present an in-depth account of company practices in employment and promotion of women to managerial positions, as well as detailed personal attitudes of male and female executives toward acceptance of women in management.

Notes

1. Kiplinger letter, *Changing Times* (April 1967), p. 15.

2. Ibid. (Based on statistics compiled by the National Education Association.)

3. There has been widespread compliance with the law, as evidenced by a study made by Prentice-Hall noting that three out of ten companies had promulgated changes in their personnel policies within one year of the enactment of the legislation. "The Labor Month in Review. Sex and Equal Opportunity Rights," *Monthly Labor Review*, August 1967. p. III.

4. Not all legislation has created greater opportunity for women. The Equal Employment Opportunity Commission has had 90 percent of its complaints by women against dismissal because of laws restricting the number of hours per week they could work.

5. Clare Booth Luce, "Is It NOW or Never for Women?" *McCalls*, April 1967, p. 49.

6. The questionnaire is appended to the report.

7. The authors deplore the non-cooperative posture of these major corporations since they benefit equally with the cooperating firms from the fruits of research on management practices.

8. To simplify subsequent tables and figures, only two categories of size will be used. Large organizations are defined as those having over 500 employees and small as having fewer than 500.

2 Incidence of Women in Managerial Positions

In the previous chapter we utilized income figures as a means of determining the incidence of women in managerial positions. The figure of less than 1 percent of women in this category compared to over 13 percent of men is abysmally low in the aggregate; but are there some industries or government agencies where the incidence (of women in these positions) is much greater? Are there deep-set obstacles to the promotion of women as practiced in company and organizational hiring and promotional policies ¡

The first section of the mail questionnaire was structured to be answered by the director of personnel or equivalent in the responding companies to provide information on the incidence of women in managerial positions and the prevailing company attitudes toward the hiring and promotion of women.

Percentage of Managerial Positions Held by Women

The proportion of managerial positions held by women was stabilized at approximately 2 percent between 1950 and 1960, according to a major survey of readers of the **Harvard Business Review.** [2] The results of our questionnaire showed that more than 70 percent of the companies responding had over 3 percent of their managerial positions held by women, as shown in Figure 3.

Little appreciable difference in the incidence of women in management existed between large and small companies:

Percent of Women in Managerial Positions	Small Organizations	Large Organizations
Under 3 %	28 %	24 %
3%to 10 %	51 %	54 %
Over 10 %	21 %	22 %

In the largest of firms, employing between 20,000 and 50,000, 33 percent of the firms had more than 10 percent of managerial positions filled by women. It would seem that more opportunities for women aspiring to managerial positions are to be found in large firms than in small. This conclusion does not agree with the **Harvard Business Review** study which concluded that although size of firm was not significant, greater opportunities for women existed in small firms. [3]

To determine whether certain industries or government agencies had a higher incidence of women in managerial positions, the survey results were cross tabulated by industry as presented in Figures 4 to 7.

A comparison of Figures 4 to 7 shows a disparity of practices within each industry classification on the utilization of women for managerial positions. Government, banking, and merchandising presented the

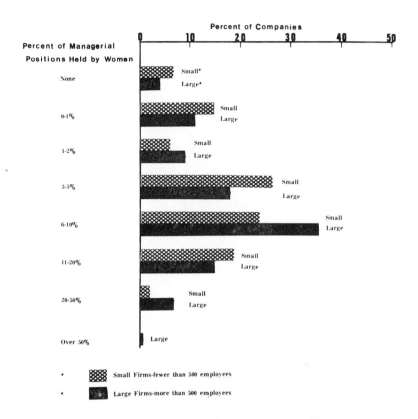

Figure 3
Percentage of Management Positions Held by Women
by Size of Company

greatest opportunities for women with 14 percent, 6 percent, and 8 percent respectively of the organizations employing women in more than 20 percent of managerial positions.[4] Insurance offered the least incentive to women, with fewer than 1 percent of managerial positions held by women; no organizations reported that women filled 20 percent of managerial ranks. Similarly, transportation and utilities did not utilize women as managers to any great degree. The percentage of firms in merchandising and banking utilizing women for 20 to 50 percent of managerial positions was three times greater than for manufacturing firms.

Figure 4
Percent of Manufacturing Firms
Utilizing Women in Managerial Positions

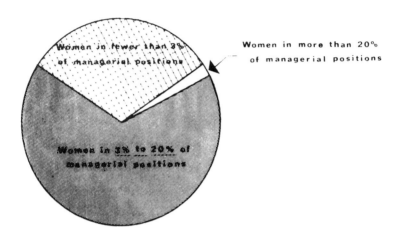

Women in fewer than 3% of managerial positions

Women in more than 20% of managerial positions

Women in 3% to 20% of managerial positions

Figure 5
Percent of Merchandising Firms
Utilizing Women in Managerial Positions

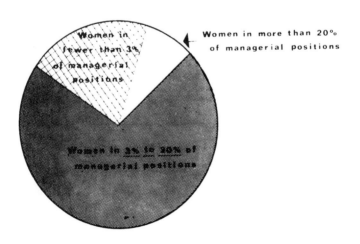

Women in fewer than 3% of managerial positions

Women in more than 20% of managerial positions

Women in 3% to 20% of managerial positions

Figure 6
Percent of Banking Firms
Utilizing Women in Managerial Positions

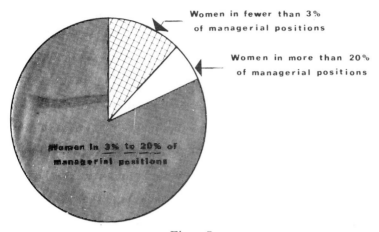

Women in fewer than 3% of managerial positions

Women in more than 20% of managerial positions

Women in 3% to 20% of managerial positions

Figure 7
Percent of Government Agencies
Utilizing Women in Managerial Positions

Women in fewer than 3% of managerial positions

Women in more than 20% of managerial positions

Women in 3% to 20% of managerial positions

Significant geographical differences do exist in the utilization of women in management. In the West women hold 11 to 20 percent of all managerial positions in one out of four companies, as noted in Figure 8. Thirty percent of the firms in which the proportion of the managerial positions held by women was double that for the country as a whole were located in the East. But in the Midwest some 25 percent of the firms had fewer than 1 percent of managerial positions filled by women.

Figure 8
Percentage of Management Positions Held by Women
By Geographical Region

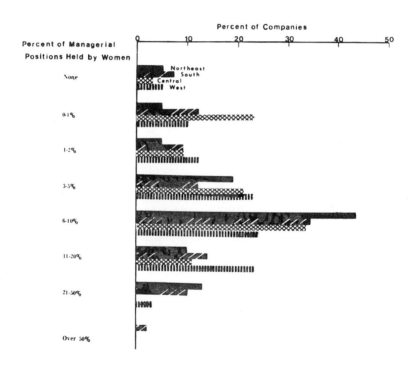

Managerial Positions Held by Women

Seventy-five percent of the respondent companies utilized women in office managerial positions or personnel management, which were the most common types of management positions held by women, as can be seen in Figure 9. Since three out of every five women in the labor force are employed in white-collar, clerical jobs, it is only to be expected that the opportunities for women for managerial positions are much greater in the office.[5] To some extent women are utilized also as staff specialists or professionals but rarely in policy making executive positions, as indicated in Figure 9.

The types of managerial positions held by women, broken down by industry classifications in Figure 10, were still primarily office management, particularly in merchandising firms and government agencies. Strangely enough, some 40 percent of the insurance companies and 30 percent of the manufacturers utilized no women in office managerial positions.

In 55 percent of the companies, staff or professional positions in management were held by women. In 83 percent of the government agencies, women were utilized in staff or professional managerial positions, compared to some 50 percent of the firms in the private sector. Other studies have concluded that there is a high degree of concentration in areas generally considered to be "women's occupations," such as welfare, public health, juvenile agencies, and other activities related to the social sciences.[6]

Further examination of Figures 9 and 10 will reveal the minimal participation of women in production and marketing supervision.

Only one out of four manufacturers utilized women in these positions. The impact on job growth caused by the tremendous advances in technology of production during

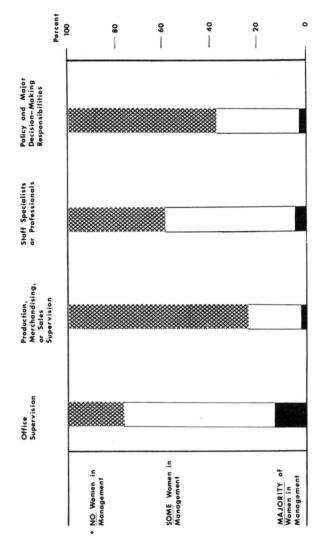

Figure 9
Types and Incidence of Management
Positions Held by Women

* - Includes "no responses."

Figure 10
Types of Management Positions Held by Women
by Industry

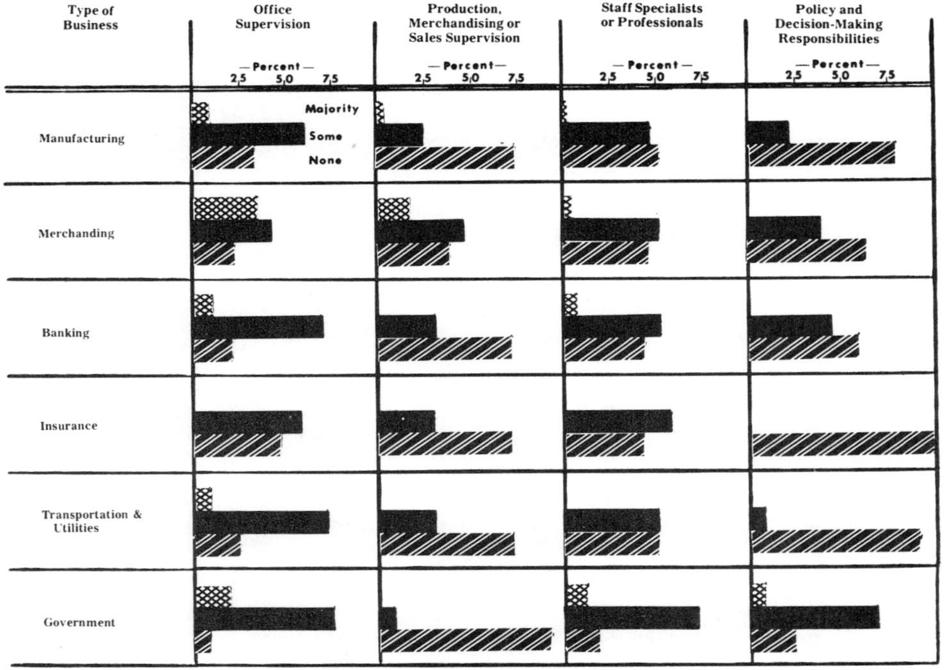

the past twenty years has been felt in the pattern of occupational distribution for both men and women. The need for workers has shifted from goods-producing to service-producing industries, as evidenced by the decline in the number of blue-collar workers in manufacturing dropping from 50 percent to 40 percent between 1947 and 1967.[7] The belief expressed by businessmen polled in the Harvard study was, "Women have little or no opportunity in those areas which are generally supposed to have least growth potential in an era of technological change."[8] Women's exclusion from the production management ranks can be attributed in large part to their inexperience and training in the new technologies. The female production manager of a small tool company interviewed during the pilot study claimed her success was due to having "grown up in the business." But she also commented that she had inadequate prior training in the technologies required for her job.

A somewhat more optimistic picture was found in merchandising firms, where some 62 percent of the companies employed women in marketing management.

Women in Policy Making Executive Positions

With the exception of government agencies, with 75 percent having women in policy making positions, women rarely reach the higher levels of management. Fewer than one firm in four utilized women in upper management echelons.

Examples of outstanding women who have reached positions of major responsibility can be found in every area of business. But the very fact that "examples" exist emphasizes the meager proportion. In the dental and medical professions women predominate as hygienists and nurses, but less than 10 percent are doctors. Statistics show that half of department store executives are women as well as 25 percent of insurance and 10 percent of

28

banking executives, but insignificant numbers are "real" executives, those in positions of high authority.[9] In spite of the recently increased proportion of women in all types of industries, the proportion at or near the top has remained essentially unchanged, about 2 percent.

Findings of the survey, as reported earlier in this chapter, indicated a somewhat greater acceptance of women as managers in large firms than small. This was again borne out in tabulations showing the percentage of firms with no women in the designated areas of management.

To a degree, the figures in the chart below show that the larger the company, the greater the proportion of women in management. However, conflicting evidence, at least for women in higher echelons of management, was found in the Harvard study. When commenting on their women respondents who were board chairmen, presidents, owner-managers, or executive vice-presidents of their firms, the report states, "The most interesting characteristic of their companies was their generally small size—over two-thirds were companies with under 100 employees, and only 2 woman-led firms had over 1,000 workers."[10]

No Women in Management				
	Small (up to 500)	Mod. Large (500-5,000)	Large (5,000-20,000)	Very Large (over 20,000)
Office Mgmt.	47 %	26 %	0 %	12 %
Production, Merchandising, Sales Mgmt.	79 %	57 %	66 %	50 %
Staff Specialists	55 %	37 %	16 %	19 %
Upper Levels of Mgmt.	78 %	55 %	38 %	69 %

Numerous reasons lie behind the exclusion of women from management ranks. The rationale behind company policies and individual attitudes, whether substantive or opinionated, is discussed in later portions of this report.

Notes

1. The accent is on the word practiced since it is most unlikely that a company would promulgate any discriminatory practices in its personnel policies.

2. G. W. Bowman et al, "Are Women Executives People" *Harvard Business Review,* July August 1965, pp. 14-28.

3. Ibid. Biases exist both in the Harvard study and this study since the former polled only *Harvard Business Review* readers and the latter may have received responses only from those firms with women in managerial positions.

4. Report of the President's Commission on the Status of Women, *American Women* (Washington, D. C.: U. S. Government Printing Office, 1963) concludes that most women in the civil service held lower grade classifications. At the time of the Civil Rights Legislation in 1964, women held about 70 percent of the grade 5 jobs and with each successively higher grade classification the proportion of jobs held by women diminished significantly.

5. Vera C. Perella, "Women and the Labor Force," *Monthly Labor Review*, February 1968, pp. 1-19.

6. Beverly Benner Cassara (ed.), *American Women: The Changing Image* (Boston: Beacon Press, 1962), passim. Although fewer than 4 percent of lawyers are women, the proportion in Federal agencies is 5 percent, and in the U.S. Department of Justice it is almost 7 percent.

7. Perella, op. cit.

8. Bowman et al, op. cit., p. 24.

9. Marilyn Mercer, "Women At Work: Is There Room at the Top?" *The Saturday Evening Post*, July 27, 1968, pp. 17-21.

10. Bowman et al, op. cit., p. 170.

3   Positive Company Attitudes Toward Women in Management

The evidence from this and other studies is that women rarely attain true managerial positions much above the rank of first line supervisor. To ascertain why women are not utilized for managerial positions, male and female respondents were asked a series of questions pertaining to the effects of marriage and legislation on promotion, the acceptance of women back into the labor force after their children are grown, etc. The purpose was to identify the reasons why more women are not promoted to managerial jobs.

Effects of Marriage and Legislation

In an effort to explore company attitudes and practices concerning the promotability of women in regard to childbearing and legislation on working hours, personnel directors were asked:

    1. Does **your firm** normally fail to promote women

to managerial positions because they are likely to marry, have children, and therefore leave the firm?

2. Does the legislation for a restricted work pattern restrain **your firm** from promoting women to management positions?

The answer to both of these issues, as shown in Figure 11, was an emphatic "no." In the view of the vast majority of companies responding to this survey, woman's biological role is not a deterrent to her entrance into the executive suite. No more than 15 percent of firms in any one industry would refuse to promote a single woman on the grounds she might marry and quit work. No doubt experience has proven this to be only one of many reasons for voluntary termination.

It should be remembered that information gathered in this portion of the study related strictly to company practices and not individual opinions. Figure 11 presents the results from all firms in each industry regardless of whether the responding executive was male or female. A point of interest here is the general agreement found in responses from both questionnaires. The only exception was evidenced from banks, where 19 percent of those employing the male respondent versus 7 percent of banks from which the respondent was a woman said "no." The report of the Equal Employment Opportunity Commission, May 1967, indicates that very few women say they are not hired or that they have been fired because they marry or because they have children. Thus, to some extent, the old view that family responsibilities would interfere with a woman's work has apparently been discarded. Also, there is some indication in this decade of greater labor force participation of women with pre-school age children. Statistics show a 6 to 10 percent rise (percent depending on age of mother) between 1960 and 1967 of working women with children under 6 years of age.[1] Although these data apply to all married women in the

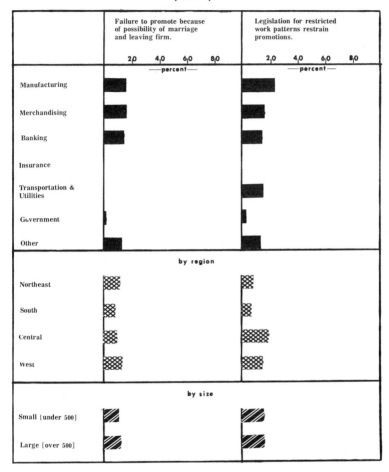

Figure 11
Effects of Marriage and Legislation on Promotion of Women

by industry

labor force, results of this survey tend to support the view that simply because a woman is single is not an impediment to her consideration for advancement.

More than three-fourths of the survey firms felt that legislation limiting work hours of women did not adversely affect a woman's chances for advancement. Even in manufacturing, where the proportion of female to male managers was low, only 22 percent of firms reported that restrictions on women's work hours had a negative effect on their promotion. Not one of the insurance companies and only 3 percent of government bureaus indicated women were held back because of the work time limitation laws.

Status of Women Re-entering the Labor Market

As previously mentioned, there is evidence that the proportion of working women in the 45 to 54 year age group has risen and will continue to rise at an accelerated pace. It has been projected that the female labor force in 1980 will total about 32 million, more than half again as large as it was in 1960. Much of the growth is expected to be among married women and there is reason to believe that the proportion of married women whose years of child-bearing and family-rearing are behind them will continue to constitute a large percentage of the female employment ranks. In an effort to determine the attitudes of responding firms toward women re-entering the labor market, personnel directors were asked to reply to the following question: "When a woman has returned to the labor market after raising a family, and has equivalent qualifications to male applicants, would your firm normally consider her as a potential manager?"

Acceptance of Women as Managers

Results of the "yes" answers, together with the reasons for acceptance of women, are presented in Figure 12, classified by type of business and geographical region. The percentages shown for responses to the various reasons are based on the number of "yes" respondents. In most instances, the sum of percentages for any one industry exceeds 100 percent, due to the fact that personnel departments chose more than one reason.

The greatest opportunities for qualified women re-entering the labor market were in civil service. In more than 90 percent of the agencies, women had equal opportunity with male applicants. It is not surprising that government agencies should head the list in non-discriminative practices. Certainly the magnitude and importance of the problems surrounding women in business were brought to light during the tenure of President Kennedy, by his appointment of the Presiaent's Commission on the Status of Women. In **American Women,** the report of the Commission's survey published in 1963, President Kennedy is quoted as saying, "We are at the beginning of an era when...men and women everywhere will have it within their power to develop their potential capacities to the maximum."

The Civil Rights legislation which followed in 1964 prohibiting discrimination in employment by reason of sex, among other things, paved the way for women to seek and receive greater acceptance into positions of authority. Evidence derived from this survey and other literature in the field point to the strict adherence to the letter of the law by government agencies. It will be interesting to watch the effects of the most recent Federal legislation in the area of discrimination against older women returning to the labor market after their children are grown. As of June 12, 1968, companies dealing in interstate commerce and which employ 100 or more workers are prohibited from discrimination by reason of age of applicant.

Sixty-one percent of merchandising firms and 71 percent of banks reported women had an equal chance with men. On the other hand, results from manufacturing, insurance, transportation, and public utility industries showed that firms in which sex of applicant was not a consideration were definitely in the minority. Only one in every five insurance companies would hire a woman who was

Figure 12

Consideration of Women as Potential Managers (Positive Factors)

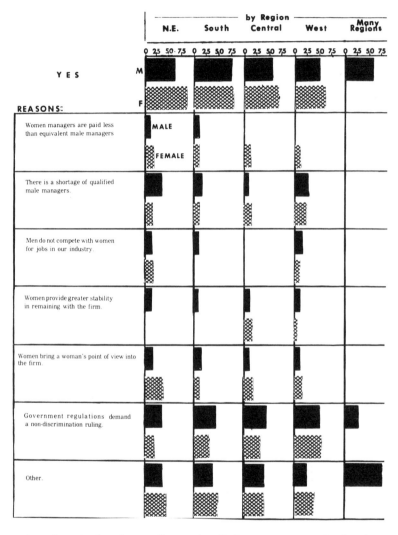

returning to business for potential management. An interesting point was revealed in replies from firms in which the responding executives were female. On the whole, these firms appeared to take a more optimistic view of

Figure 12

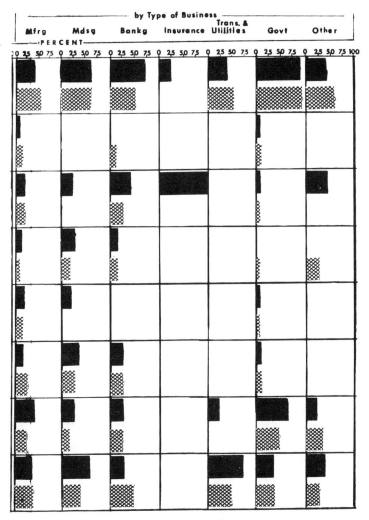

women's advancement possibilities than was evidenced from male-respondent firms. Perhaps this is a reflection of the fact that companies with successful women in management are more aware, or at least receptive to, women's capabilities.

From male-respondent firms a bare majority of those in the Midwest (53 percent), West (51 percent), and Northeast (60 percent) would consider management training for a woman who had been away from the labor market a number of years. Women had equal opportunity with their male counterparts in three out of four male-respondent companies located in the South and nine out of ten of those with female respondents.

Although data from previous portions of the questionnaire revealed a somewhat greater number of women managers in large firms than small, there was little difference by size of firm in regard to equal opportunity for women returning to work when family responsibilities have lessened.

	Small Firms	Large Firms
Positive company policy of male respondents in promoting women returning to the labor force.	54 %	61 %
Positive company policy of female respondents in promoting women returning to the labor force.	76 %	68 %

Comparison between male- and female-respondent firms indicates that those with women executives are more likely to have favorable attitudes about promoting and training women returning to the labor market later in life. The questionnaire contained a list of specific reasons why a firm might have favorable attitudes toward women rejoining the labor market, and provided additional space for write-in comments. The verbation remarks contribute valuable supplementary data and add insight into personal values and attitudes.

Women Paid Less than Men

One of the possible reasons advanced in the questionnaire for the acceptance of women rejoining the labor market was, "Do companies pay their women managers less than equivalent male managers?" Fewer than 3 percent of male-responding firms in any industry said sex made a difference in salary structure. The same general reaction came from female-responding firms, but to a somewhat lesser degree—13 percent of banks, 11 percent of manufacturers and 11 percent of government agencies said women were in fact paid less. This suggests the possibility that were a man to hold the position of the woman executive responding to the later portion of the questionnaire, he might be in a higher salary bracket.

Tabulations by size showed that small companies were the only ones citing economic discrimination as a factor in employment of women. Apparently smaller firms find it possible to improvise or assign a less important job title to women-held positions to account for clear-cut pay differences. In spite of the low proportion of companies in which women's pay was less, literature abounds with actual cases of lack of salary conformity between the sexes. A survey made by the Federal Equal Employment Opportunity Commission disclosing that many career women accepted subordinate pay without protest was quoted in **Newsweek** magazine:

> It found, for instance, that one large Midwestern manufacturer was paying a female branch manager half the salary it was giving the five men who were running similar branches—but the woman didn't complain because she was afraid of jeopardizing her job.[3]

Similar examples of pay discrimination have been uncovered by authors writing for **Seventeen** and the **Saturday Evening Post:**

> Prejudice against women does exist, though it's less widespread and more subtle than in mother's day. Today although women are

less likely to be excluded from certain occupations they are likely to be paid less than men for the same kind of work.[4]

The man I replaced was called production director, but I'm called production manager. The work is identical, but somehow production manager pays $4,000 less a year than production director did.[5]

Shortage of Qualified Men

Another reason advanced in the questionnaire was that women were considered for potential management only because of a shortage of qualified men. The survey results showed that small percentages of firms in most industries felt this was a deciding factor. A notable exception was seen in replies from insurance companies, only 20 percent of which would consider management training for a woman, and then only because there was a shortage of male managers. The drain of American manpower into the Armed Services and the greater numbers of men enrolled in advanced, post-graduate work to meet the increasing demands for technological expertise have resulted in a shortage of qualified male applicants for many industries. However, it should be encouraging to women that few companies give "shortage of males" as a reason for accepting females into positions of responsibility.

No Competition from Men

To determine further the reasons for acceptance of women, the questionnaire asked if a married woman who has not worked for a number of years and is now returning to the business world has an opportunity for management because men offer no competition in certain industries. Data collected from this survey confirm the results of many studies, that there is keen competition between the sexes for most jobs. Even in replies from merchandising firms, only one in four reported men did not vie with women for management positions. Size of firm appeared to have some bearing on competition. Returns from 14 percent of small companies (500 or fewer employees) who would consider a woman said, "Yes, men don't compete," compared to 4 percent of firms with up to 20,000 and none of the giant corporations.

Today there is a shortage of management personnel which has forced many companies to explore all avenues for qualified applicants, regardless of sex. The growing demands for highly trained people in government service and the teaching profession will continue to drain the labor market of potential management personnel for industry. Commenting on the changing personal values of so many of this generation's young men which significantly influence choice of careers, one writer states:

> Businessmen are aware that the brightest young men are being drawn to fields where they feel they can "contribute to society." The contribution that industry makes to society is hard to explain to undergraduates; and unfair as it may be, the hard fact is that the profit motive is without honor in the minds of a lot of upcoming talent.[6]

Nonetheless, in spite of increasing recognition by industries that they will have to draw upon more and more women to fill key jobs, there is still a great deal of competition by men. Company policies reflect the attitudes of society in general as well as their managers. These attitudes are also reflective of men in lower levels of management who strongly object to being bypassed by women. The report of the Harvard study supports this view as follows:

> So we find resentment on the part of many younger men, who consider the growing presence in management of married women—who "do not need to work"—as a block to their own advancement.[7]

Greater Stability in Women Managers

Most firms rejected the statement, "women provide greater stability in remaining with the firm." Apparently the experience of the majority has been that executive mobility is not directly related to sex. An interesting observation in this connection appeared in returns from merchandising firms. None of the female-respondent companies thought women remained with the company longer than men, but 18 percent of the male-respondent firms did.

In this era of male mobility, not only in the total labor force but to a high degree in male executives, it might be expected that women who return to the business world with sufficient capabilities and motivation to seek and receive positions of responsibility would evidence greater permanency in their jobs than men. The proportion of college-bred married women between the ages of forty-five and fifty-four rose to an unprecedented 61 percent in 1966.[8] Yet, aside from purely economic necessity, many women return to work for a variety of reasons, not the least of which are to seek wider horizons and to escape boredom. These women, unlike most men, choose whether they want to work and how long they wish to remain working. However, an examination of existing literature reveals that very little is known about their reasons for leaving, but this survey's findings indicate little difference in turn-over rates between men and women.

Utilizing a Woman's Point of View

Is the fact that a woman brings "a woman's point of view" into the company a contributing factor in her consideration for management? On the basis of firms in industries where women had equal opportunity with their male counterparts, only one in three merchandising companies and one in four banks felt this quality of women worked in their favor. Since women in America do the largest share of buying and usually pay the bills and control the family budget, it is understandable that women executives would have potentially greater insights and opportunities in merchandising and financial institutions. However, bringing a woman's point of view into manufacturing, insurance, transportation, and public utility firms appeared completely unnecessary. It is somewhat surprising that so few government agencies (9 percent) felt this attribute to be needed, when considering the large number of health and welfare agencies and the relatively high percentage of women managers in this social services oriented work.

Effects of Legislation on Promotional Practices

Company attitudes reported earlier regarding the effects of Federal legislation on women's opportunities were again emphasized when a similar statement was listed on the questionnaire as a possible reason for hiring a woman whose qualifications were equivalent to those of a male applicant. Despite the low proportion of firms in most industries (about 30 percent) which cited the inclusion of sex in the Civil Rights legislation as contributing to the status of women, the important point is the fairly uniform distribution of responses throughout all types of businesses, except insurance (note that women had a chance in a few insurance companies only because of the shortage of men).

This percentage appears to confirm the findings of the Prentice-Hall study, previously noted, which disclosed that three out of ten companies had made personnel policy changes in accordance with the provisions of the law. To a degree, the crusade for equality of opportunity has been advanced through legislative action, but the law per se has not proven to be the vehicle for reaching women's ultimate goal. Although strict adherence to the law would be expected from government employers (95 percent did say women had equal employment opportunities with male applicants), the Civil Rights Act was a consideration in only 67 percent of the male-respondent agencies and 49 percent of the female-respondent offices.

In commenting on the removal of government agencies' authority to request men only, by reason of the Civil Rights Act, Mr. John W. Macy, Jr. of the U. S. Civil Service Commission in a speech before the Business and Professional Women's Organization said, "In 1965, 29 percent of the eligibles (from Federal Service Entrance Examinations) certified to appointing officers were women, and women received nearly 27 percent of the appointments. In contrast, during the twelve months ending October 1961, less than 15 percent of the appointments from the FSEE went to women."[9] Mr. Macy also points to the progress of women in higher levels of Federal Service, by reporting that 3,500 women were appointed or promoted to positions at salaries of $10,600 or more during January 1965 and October 1965. "Many of those appointments represent breakthroughs into occupations formerly held exclusively or almost exclusively by men."[10]

In spite of this undisputed triumph for women in government service, negative attitudes still persist in the world of business. Results similar to those of this survey were disclosed in the report of the Harvard study: "As many as 61 percent of the men and 47 percent of the women are of the opinion that the business community will never wholly accept women executives no matter how many laws are passed."[11]

An additional point of interest is the relationship of size of firm to observance of the law. Tabulations show a considerably greater proportion of large firms (47 percent) than small (14 percent) in which government controls have a decided bearing on the employment of women managers.

Positive company attitudes toward the acceptance of women in management were generally restricted to merchandishing firms and banking institutions. In the case of manufacturing, insurance, transportation, and public utility firms, it could be considered that there was a negative attitude toward women in management. The next chapter examines this negative attitude in depth.

Notes

1. Vera C. Perella, "Women and the Labor Force," *Monthly Labor Review*, February 1968, pp. 1-19.

2. Ibid

3. *Newsweek*, June 27, 1966, p. 76.

4. David Klein, "How Much of a Man's World Is It?" *Seventeen*, November 1967, p. 216.

5. Marilyn Mercer, "Women at Work: Is There Room at the Top?" *The Saturday Evening Post*, July 27 1968, p. 18.

6. Ibid, p. 60.

7. G. W. Bowman et al, "Are Women Executives People?" *Harvard Business Review*, July August 1965, p. 26.

8. John B. Parrish and Jean S. Block, "The Future for Women in Science and Engineering," *Bulletin of the Atomic Scientists*, May 1968, p. 49.

9. John W. Macy, Jr., "Unless We Begin Now," *Vital Speeches of the Day*, September 1, 1966, p. 679.

10. Ibid.

11. Bowman, op cit., p. 19.

4 Negative Company Attitudes Toward Women in Management

Although the majority of companies in most industries expressed willingness to permit women in the management ranks, those which totally rejected females appeared to be vehement in their opposition, especially firms from which the responding executives were men. Figure 13 shows the percentage of negative responses and reasons for exclusion of women, classified by type of business and geographical region.

An Appraisal of Women in Management

None of the statements listed on the questionnaire could be construed as being dogmatic or prejudicial in nature. Therefore the high proportion of firms giving more than one reason for considering women unsuitable for management is significant. It seems logical to assume that many organizations felt there was sound rationale behind their attitudes or, at least, felt the need to justify their negativism. However, analysis of the "write-ins" disclosed that there is discrimination against women still prevalent in the business community, which may reflect individual attitudes.

Age and Training

Most companies today spend thousands of dollars in management development programs in the expectation of improving the managerial effectiveness of those persons responsible for the operations of the business. However, results are frequently realized only after long periods of training and employers naturally place great emphasis on selecting applicants with the highest possible potential. Age of prospective managers plays a significant part in the selection process. Although the proportion of older women entering the labor market the "second time around" has been steadily on the increase and many are college graduates with special qualities to recommend them, they often experience the frustration of being "too old" to be considered for management training. The problem often encountered by this group of women is that industries offer them menial, unchallenging jobs which they find unacceptable.

In an article concerning manpower shortage and its relation to business proliferation and the increasing need to search for talent among all groups, the writer states:

> Personnel and industrial relations in most companies now are narrowly limited by a devotion to statistics and the immediate outlook. A reorientation toward human relations is required, with the elimination of such outdated attitudes as discrimination against older workers, minorities and women.[1]

Employers in our survey, however, expressed a more optimistic view. Age was not considered a barrier to women's advancement possibilities in at least two of every three firms (nine of ten manufacturers).

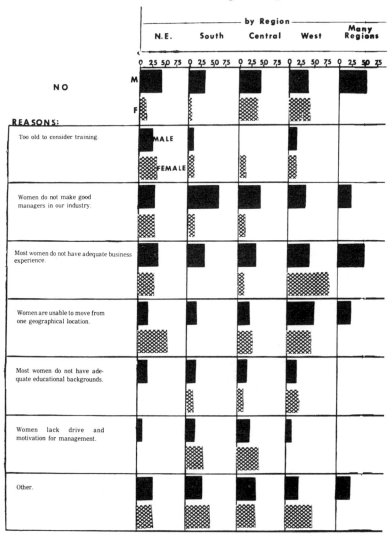

Figure 13
Consideration of Women as Potential Managers (Negative Factors)

Effectiveness of Women as Managers

Another important factor influencing company attitudes toward women as candidates for training is the per-

Figure 13

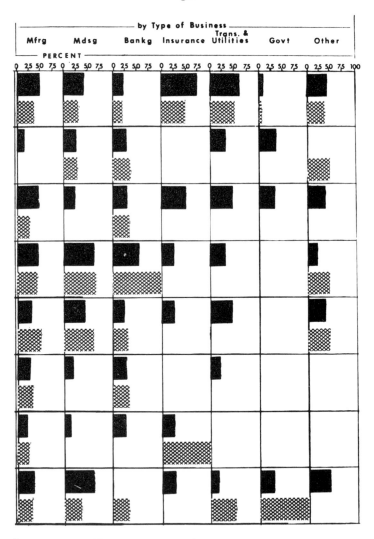

formance effectiveness of those women already in executive positions. In probing into this area, employers were asked to affirm or deny the statement: "Women do not make good managers in our company." Although all firms in our study employed some women in management, the significant fact revealed in the answers to this statement is the generally favorable attitude of firms where the responding executive was female and the widespread opposition from those in which a male member of management was the respondent. Later portions of the questionnaire delve into personal attitudes of businessmen and women, but in this particular instance the question was limited to company reactions.

The difference in outlook between firms in this survey seems to support the conclusion that companies which have had experience with successful female executives have a greater tendency to be favorable in their appraisement of women managers. Literature in the field relating personal working experience of executives with evaluation of women in management appears to reinforce company attitudes. The Harvard study found, "Those (executives) who report actual working experience with women managers are most likely to be strongly favorable to women in management than their colleagues lacking such experience."[2]

Whether women possess natural characteristics or unique personality traits which, in fact, handicap them to the extent evidenced by so many "male" firms (who defined them as "not good managers") is discussed in later portions of this report.

Once again, tabulations by size of responding firm appear to add emphasis to earlier conclusions that large firms in this survey offered greater opportunities for women managers than small companies.

	Male-Respondent Firms	
"Women do not make good managers in our company."	Large 33 %	Small 59 %

The majority of small companies indicated unfavorable experiences with their female managers, as opposed to only one in three of large employers.

Inadequacy of Women's Business Experience

Turning now to more specific issues, the next statement responded to by firms refusing to consider management training for a woman re-entering the business world was: "Most women do not have adequate business experience." By and large, women agree with men that the years away from the labor force while rearing a family have put women out of touch with the technological innovations and tremendous changes in the conduct of most firms which have taken place in recent years.

It is particularly difficult for women in staff positions to maintain professional competence when returning to work. Evidence points to the increasing rate of professional obsolescence with the explosion of scientific knowledge. One educator states, "It is estimated that if a woman scientist or engineer is away from her profession for seven to ten years the literature in her field will have doubled by her return."[3]

Speaking less specifically of professional skills and more generally of the overall effects on business management caused by technological changes, another professor commented, "The speed of technical advance has been so great that even the best brains can scarcely keep up with it."[4]

A high proportion of business firms, as can be seen in Figure 13, agreed that long years of absence hindered even the "qualified" woman from being admitted into management training. In the specific instances of banking and merchandising firms, traditionally considered to be women's fields, large numbers of firms subscribed to this theory.

Lack of Geographical Mobility

Another important issue restraining many companies from hiring women for potential management is the argument that women are unable to relocate geographically. Trends toward diversification and decentralization of firms in recent years have had important effects on the opportunities of working women, primarily married women. Many employers report they prefer male employees because the turnover rate for women is higher than for men and that hiring married women adds one more element of risk because the family residence is normally determined by the occupation of the husband.[5]

Our culture segregates the sexes into two distinct roles: the husband as the breadwinner, and the wife as the helper. Although one in every ten households is headed by a woman, in the remaining 90 percent women are usually secondary earners and if the husband's career opportunities require moving to a new area the wife must leave her job. Studies made by the U.S. Department of Labor show that the higher the education and skill level of men, the higher the migration rate and that among men who migrate, half give job-related reasons for the move.[6]

Since available literature does not indicate the extent of migration when two jobs in a family are involved in the move, our questionnaire sought to determine if a married woman's inability to relocate to a different geographical area was a factor in her exclusion from management. This question was directed toward consideration of older women, those with qualifications equivalent to those of male applicants. It would seem that the husbands in this group would also be older, have responsible positions, and, most likely, be settled in their jobs. Therefore, it is significant that substantial numbers of firms in all industries, except government, would fail to hire such a woman on the grounds she could not relocate. Yet this negative attitude appears understandable, particularly for the older woman, since her husband would be reluctant to quit his position for the sake of her career. Results of our study show a greater percentage of female-respondent employers of firms in several industries supported this view.

Male (M) and Female (F) Respondent Firms	Manufacturing		Merchandising		Banking	
	M	F	M	F	M.	F
"Women are unable to move from one geographical location."	29 %	50 %	38 %	67 %	25 %	33 %

Interestingly enough, a greater proportion of female-respondent firms felt that the inability of women to relocate geographically was a deterrent to promotion than male-respondent firms. Judging from the fact that women had greater opportunities for promotion in female-respondent companies (see "No" responses, Figure 13) it would seem that these firms had experienced greater evidence of women's inability to relocate.

Inadequacy of Women's Educational Qualifications

Responses to the next reason submitted to firms refusing to hire a woman for management training indicate rather contradictory results from what might be expected. Few firms in any industries answered affirmatively to the statement, "Most women do not have adequate educational backgrounds." It would appear that women seeking managerial posts in most of the surveyed companies did have sufficient education.

Other studies point out that women have not made a strong commitment to higher education. Our culture incapacitates women for business careers and guides girls into training for parenthood and homemaking. However, attitudes of American society today show definite changes toward family emphasis on college education for daughters as well as sons. The tremendous increase in the proportion of women in the labor force the past two decades can be directly traced to the importance placed on educational attainment. Moreover, the participation of working married women tends to increase in direct proportion to level of schooling.

Although the percentage of girls who enter college immediately after high school is steadily rising, the proportion of female to male graduates has remained about the same, because the numbers of men with college degrees have been increasing at a much faster rate. Demands in this era of scientific advancements have forced men to obtain greater academic training, and statistics show that the higher the educational level, the farther behind women fall. One author writes, "The most alarming aspect of this situation is that it is getting worse; women obtained 40 percent of all master's degrees and other second-level degrees in 1930, but only 31 percent in 1963."[7]

The fact remains that the absolute number of women with college degrees has risen, but whether women accept the challenge to seek the additional education and training necessary for executive positions will have significant impact on their goals toward equality with men.

The questionnaire results were that few firms in any industries felt women had less adequate educational backgrounds than men applicants. It is interesting that a somewhat greater percentage of female-respondent firms than male-respondent firms in manufacturing and banking preferred men because of their higher education. Once again, this may reflect past experience with women managers. Later portions of this report are concerned with profiles of the responding executives and show comparisons in educational level between the respondent sexes.

Women Lack Drive and Motivation for Managements

Another important argument advanced by employers as reason for excluding women is that women lack drive and motivation for managements. Results of this survey confirm to some degree the findings of other studies. In the opinion of one in six manufacturing and merchandising firms and one in four banking and insurance companies, women were refused admission to management because they do not have the determination necessary to meet the demands of business management.

A common denominator found in most successful women is their exceptionally strong motivation. They find their business life stimulating and absorbing. Yet a very real problem exists for the woman trying to juggle the responsibilities of a family, even when the children are grown, with the demands of a professional or executive career. Because a woman cannot usually pursue a career with the single-mindedness of a man, we find a high proportion of single or divorced women among female top executives. Many highly educated, capable women approve of high-ranking positions for other women but have no desire to become involved in the long-term commitment for themselves.

The statement that women in general are not career oriented seems well founded. Evidence derived from the Harvard study reveals that 82 percent of male executives and 76 percent of female executives surveyed supported the view that women themselves were responsible for persisting negative attitudes, because "they have accepted their exclusion from management ranks without major protest."[8]

Company attitudes in our study did not disclose the intensity of negativism shown by the Harvard study, but do support the conclusion that women themselves are responsible for much of the so-called prejudicial treatment.

The evidence from this and other similar studies is that there are distinct company attitudes that tend to disfavor the utilization of women in management. Many of these attitudes are based upon individual company experience and reflect a realistic appraisal of a dollar-and-cents evaluation. But other attitudes reflect a deep seated bias or prejudice against women in management by men in particular. To document these attitudes, our questionnaire polled the male and female respondents separately. These results are presented in the subsequent chapters of this report.

Notes

1. John Tebbel, "People and Jobs," *Saturday Review* December 30, 1967, p. 42.

2. G. W. Bowman et al, "Are Women Executives People?" *Harvard Business Review,* July /August 1965, p. 166.

3. John B. Parrish and Jean S. Block, "The Future for Women in Science and Engineering, *"Bulletin of the Atomic Scientists,* May 1968, p. 48.

4. Tebbel, op. cit., p. 9.

5. Beverly Benner Cassara (ed.), *American Women: The Changing Image* (Boston: Beacon Press, 1962), p. 29.

6. Vera C. Perella, "Women and the Labor Force," *Monthly Labor Review,* February 1968, p. 8.

7. John W. Macy, Jr., "Unless We Begin Now," *Vital Speeches of the Day,* September 1, 1966, p. 680.

8. Bowman, op. cit., p. 164.

5 Profiles of Respondents

To obtain an understanding of the reactions to acceptance or rejection of women managers from the viewpoint of successful executives themselves, the remaining sections of the two questionnaires mailed to each firm were designed for completion by the president or other top level male member of management and by the highest ranking female executive.

It was considered a major importance to the validity of the study to solicit opinions of a representative cross-section of executives with decision making responsibilities, whose attitudes influence the present and future progress of women toward their goal of equal opportunity in the business world. This objective was achieved. Our respondents included presidents, board chairmen, executive vice-presidents, owner-managers, marketing directors, financial executives, personnel and industrial relations officers, and government officials of city, state, and Federal agencies. This chapter presents profiles of the over 300 businessmen and women who cooperated in our study.

To provide an overview of both sexes, Table 2 presents the backgrounds of respondents without regard to size of firm or type of business. Certain characteristics appear typical to both men and women executives, while other aspects show diversity of backgrounds between the sexes.

(Table 2

Age, Education, Marital Status
of Respondents

Age	Men	Women
20-29	2%	2%
30-39	15%	16%
40-49	34%	30%
50-59	35%	40%
60 & Over	10%	6%

Education	Men	Women
College degree	57%	34 %
Post-graduate degree	34%	17%

Marital Status	Men	Women
Married	89%	37%
Single	2%	40%
Divorced	0%	11%

Note: Percentages do not total 100%; remainder are "no answer".

Age, Education and Marital Status

In comparing male with female respondents, several qualities common to the entire population of American women in management were reflected again in this study. Note the higher proportion of single or divorced women (51 percent, as opposed to 2 percent of the men) and the smaller proportion with college training (34 percent, as opposed to 57 percent of the men). Age distribution for men and women was virtually identical—79 percent of men and 76 percent of women were over forty. However, as was expected, the predominance of older women, particularly those over fifty, was interrelated with educational level; the majority of those with at least four years of college were younger.

Although the absolute number of women executives in large firms (over 500 employees) exceeded those from smaller firms by a three to one margin, somewhat different characteristics were revealed between the groups.

Characteristic	Large	Small
Married	38 %	52 %
Over 50 years of Age	50 %	38 %
Post-Graduate Degrees	19 %	7 %

Note: Any apparent discrepancy between the above percentages and those shown in Table 2 is due to exclusion of "no size" returns.

Business women in small firms (as compared to those in large companies) were more likely to be married and younger, but less likely to have advanced degrees. These conclusions may be applicable to this sample only and not functions of the entire group of female executives.

Work Experience

Since human attitudes are learned through association and experience, the questionnaire sought to explore the attitudes of executives toward women based on the interrelationships between length of service in management positions and associations with women as subordinates. Table 3 presents a compilation of work experience of respondents.

The age patterns of male and female respondents were very similar, but women had considerably less management experience than men. This suggests the probability that a considerable number of female executives had advanced from non-management positions. The majority of women (59 percent) had less than twenty years' service, while almost half (48 percent) of the men had been in management more than twenty years. To a large extent this trend held true for all sizes of companies. However, in the giant corporations (those with over 20,000 employees), both men and women managers had less experience than in smaller organizations, with 70 percent having been managers less than twenty years.

Table 3

Work Experience of Respondents

Years in Management Positions

	Men	Women
Less than 10 Years	5%	31%
10 to 19 Years	34%	28%
20 to 29 Years	35%	28%
30 to 39 Years	12%	2%
Over 40 Years	1%	1%

Supervisory Experience

	Men	Women
Supervised women in non-management positions.	84%	81%
Supervised women in management positions.	64%	58%

Since respondents to this survey were usually members of middle and upper levels of management, it was expected that most would have had working experience with women as subordinates. Results show the vast majority of both male (84 percent) and female (81 percent) respondents had supervised women in non-management positions. Although the proportion of those who had supervised women in management positions dropped considerably, it is not surprising that more than half (64 percent male, 58 percent female) had been in direct charge of women supervisors, as these findings reflect the high proportion of men and women respondents in top level administrative positions. In spite of the minimal percentage of managerial positions held by women in any firms, the actual number of such positions naturally expands in ratio to size of company. It would seem logical then that the proportion of respondents who had women managers as subordinates would tend to increase in larger organizations. This assumption was validated for women executives, but contradicted to some degree for the men.

Size of Company	Men	Women
500 or Fewer	65 %	52 %
500 - 5,000	63 %	57 %
5,000 - 20,000	69 %	56 %
Over 20,000	50 %	63 %

The generally accepted premise that executives who have had experience with women managers, particularly those who have supervised them, are inclined to have favorable attitudes toward women is explored in the reactions to specific issues posed later in the questionnaire.

Family Background

Educational level and occupation of fathers of both male and female respondents showed a similar pattern as shown in Table 4.

Roughly one in four had been to college, about half held management positions and one in six were professional men. On the other hand, a greater percentage of mothers of female executives (compared to males) had college training and were in professional jobs. One out of three of these mothers were employed and 40 percent of this group were professional women, which offers some evidence of women managers coming from families with educated mothers.

As would be expected, wives and husbands of respon-

Table 4
Family Backgrounds of Respondents

Attended College	Men	Women
Father	27%	22%
Mother	18%	24%
Wife/Husband	45%	74%

	Occupation					
	Non-Supervisory Job		Management Position		Professional Job	
	Men	Women	Men	Women	Men	Women
Father	28%	28%	48%	40%	15%	16%
Mother	28%	18%	2%	3%	5%	13%
Wife/Husband	28%	8%	6%	50%	17%	42%

dents showed dissimilar patterns in both educational background and kinds of jobs. Almost half (45 percent) of the wives had attended college and half (51 percent) were working. This supports the findings of the U.S. Department of Labor studies made in recent years, which show that the level of the husband's income does not always determine whether the wife works.[1]

The husband's income is only one factor in the propensity of the wife to work. Specifically, it does not necessarily hold that the higher the husband's income, the lower the rate of working married women. In fact, the participation of married women in the business world has increased substantially in those families where the husband's income is above average. "More and more wives are going to work not because the basic necessities are lacking, but to afford a higher standard of living, to satisfy personal non-monetary aspirations, and, very probably, to assert a measure of economic self-sufficiency."[2]

Three-fourths of the husbands of women respondents (37

percent were married) were college trained and over 90 percent were in high ranking positions. Occupations of the husband and wife complemented each other. In order for the wife to be successful in her career, the husband must consider the wife's job to be an important part of her life and be sympathetic to the demands and responsibilities involved in her work.

The opinions of respondents to the human characteristics necessary for management and the suitability or unsuitability of women to meet these requirements will be discussed in the next chapter.

Notes

1. Vera C. Perella, "Women in the Labor Force," Monthly Labor Review, February 1968, p. 4.

2. Ibid., p. 5.

6 Promotability of Women to Top Management

The purpose of this study was to obtain both company and individual attitudes toward women in management. The company attitude sections, completed by the personnel department, were reflective of actual company practice in the hiring and promoting of women in managerial positions. The conclusions reached from the company attitude sections of the questionnaires were that the opportunities for women to have equal or near equal status with men for managerial and executive positions are severely limited. A series of logical reasons were provided personnel departments in the questionnaire to determine why companies failed to promote women to managerial positions.

This and subsequent chapters examine individual attitudes and opinions of both male and female managers toward women as managers. The first section of this chapter contains the compilation of attitudes toward the importance of certain personal characteristics required for top management and whether these characteristics are more commonly found in men or women. The final section of the chapter examines personal opinions of both male and female respondents on the attitudes of women to their jobs.

Characteristics of Top Management

This section of the questionnaire set forth a series of personal characteristics as requirements for upper management positions. Table 5 presents the relative ranking of such characteristics by men and women managers.

Table 5
Ranking in Importance of Certain Personal Characteristics as Requirements for Upper Management

As Seen by Men		As Seen by Women	
Decisiveness	96%	Emotional Stability	93%
Consistency and		Decisiveness	92%
Objectivity	95%	Consistency and	
Emotional Stability	94%	Objectivity	90%
Analytical Ability	93%	Analytical Ability	88%
Perception and		Perception and	
Empathy	91%	Empathy	88%
Loyalty	90%	Loyalty	87%
Interest in People	87%	Interest in People	85%
Creativity	83%	Creativity	79%
Attention to Detail	40%	Attention to Detail	31%

There was a high degree of similarity of response between men and women managers in their rating of the characteristics required for upper management. The opinions of men were supported almost unanimously by women. Slight, yet inconsequential, differences existed in the order of importance placed on the top ranking first three items, "Decisiveness," "Consistency and Objectivity," and "Emotional Stability." Men rated "Decisiveness" in first place and women put "Emotional Stability" at the top. All of the characteristics noted in Table 5 were considered important for upper management except one, "Attention to Detail." [1]

Negative attitudes toward women's place in the lower levels of management persist far less strongly than in the upper ranks. Whether women reach the top depends to a large extent on opinions in the business community of women's inherent intellectual and psychological characteristics. If women do not possess the personality traits essential to top level management, then the rationale for their exclusion appears sound. Our respondents were asked to state whether the characteristics identified in Table 5 were more likely to be found in men or in women. Figure 14 shows the proportion of respondents who answered that the characteristic was more common to women. [2]

As was expected, the stereotyped thinking about women's personality traits was confirmed by the majority of both male and female respondents. Of the eight characteristics considered essential for high ranking positions, women were said to possess four. Interestingly, these four, "Perception and Empathy," "Creativity," "Loyalty," and "Interest in People," rated fifth place or lower in the list of requirements by both men and women. The ninth item, "Attention to Detail," rejected by both sexes as essential for top executives, received overwhelming agreement as being a feminine attribute. Naturally, women tend to perceive more good qualities in their sex than men do, but results showed a striking similarity in pattern of response by both male and female managers.

Figure 14

Male and Female Attitudes Toward Women In
Upper Levels of Management
Percent of respondents perceiving certain
characteristics more common to females than males.

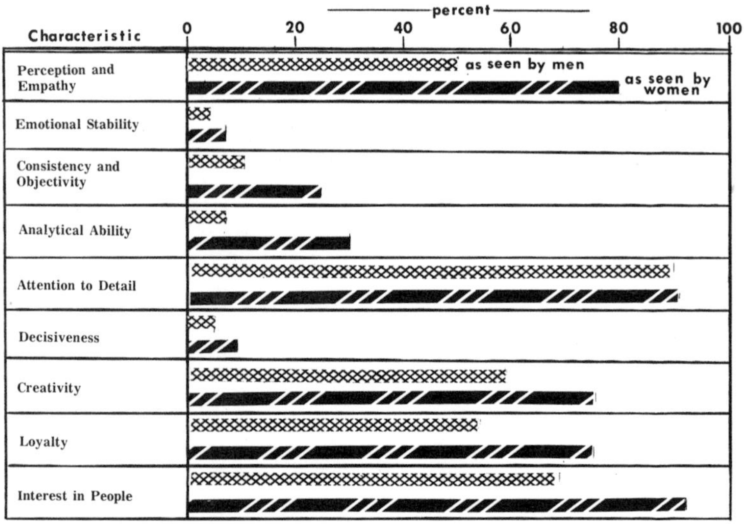

As portrayed in Figure 14, the basic difference between masculine and feminine opinions appeared to be in degree of intensity rather than in kind. However, a deviation in pattern was evidenced in response to the characteristic, "Perception and Empathy." Eighty percent of the female executives expressed the view that women were more likely to have this quality, while the male executives were divided equally in their opinions. Perhaps the variation here may be attributed to different interpretations of the term "perception," since its connotation may suggest intelligence or the quality of discernment to some, and sensitivity, insight, or intuition to others.

It has often been said that women have a flair for and deep interest in people. By nature they are understanding, sympathetic and intuitive toward others' needs. Tests made on a group of women executives by a consulting ps^vchiatrist showed they scored high in religious interests, "w.iich in a business context could mean an idealistic approach to the job."[3] It is no doubt because of these characteristics that women have been successful in responsible positions involving social work, personnel, and office administration.

A point of significance to this study, however, is shown in the opinions of the 300 undergraduate male and female students who were queried on the identical questions. Barely half (52 percent) of the men students thought that women were more perceptive and sensitive to the feelings of others than men, which is amazingly similar to the opinions of male executives.

Turning now to the qualities which predominate in men and therefore handicap women in upper levels of management, the majority of respondents agreed that men were emotionally more stable than women, that men had greater objectivity and logical reasoning ability and were definitely more confident and certain of their decisions. The same relative percentages shown for the business respondents were evidenced in the student replies. In spite of the low percentage of both boys and girls who indicated women had the advantage over men in these key qualities, it is interesting that the proportionate relationship of girl students to boy students almost paralleled the response of female to male executives.

Characteristics More Common to Women				
	Males		Females	
	Executives	Students	Executives	Students
Emotional Stability	3%	6%	6%	15%
Consistency and Objectivity	10%	10%	25%	15%
Analytical Ability	6%	10%	30%	24%
Decisiveness	4%	8%	9%	14%

Recent literature on the pros and cons of female emotionalism and feminine irrational reasoning suggests a rather curious anomaly in the attitudes of society in general and the business community in particular. Results of this study tend to support the view that women have inherent qualities that disqualify them for executive roles. Similar negativism was evidenced by over half (51 percent) of the 1,000 male executives polled by Harvard Business School, who reported women were "temperamentally unfit" for management jobs.[4]

Disagreement in attitudes is shown in other studies. The Administrative Management Society asked 1,900 business, industrial, and service organizations to give their opinions on which sex they preferred to hire for certain positions that could be performed equally well by men or women. Thirty-two percent preferred men, 33 percent preferred women, and 35 percent had no preferences. "One reason given for preferring women: Women are more stable and dependable." A reason cited for favoring men: Men are more stable and dependable.[5]

Some writers protest that women have no place in top executive ranks because they are given to jealousy, egotism, and decisions based on emotion rather than on facts or reason. On the other hand, there are those who say that men are not exempt from emotion, that they are inclined to be irritable, that they are moody and at times explosive. One author writes, "Only computers are free of feeling."[6]

If women's intrinsic mental capacity is inferior to that of men, then the fight for female acceptance into positions of authority can be challenged. It is true that few women have made strong commitments to fields requiring a high degree of analytical ability, such as engineering and science. However, the fact is that our culture has not encouraged women to develop their latent abilities. Girls are not supposed to excel in math or physics. On the other hand, the sharp increase in recent years of the number of women achieving advanced degrees in mathematics alone may mark the beginning of a substantial rise in women's participation in previously male-dominated fields. The number of Ph.D.'s in mathematics earned by women was fixed at approximately ten a year during the period 1930 to 1959. In 1960 the number rose to eighteen and by 1965 it was sixty.[7] Although this group represents an infinitesimal segment of the entire population of American women and even an extremely small proportion of the college trained women, it does appear to support the view of a district court judge who is quoted as saying, "Men have no monopoly on brains or competence and are not entitled to preferential treatment."[8]

Personal Attitudes Toward Women in Management

The last portion of our questionnaire sought to probe deeply into the reactions of managers to specific issues involved in the highly controversial subject of women's promotability to managerial positions. The questionnaire contained nineteen statements and requested the responding executives to answer "yes" or "no" to each. For purposes of analyzing the results of this survey and to correlate these findings with those of the student questionnaire, the pilot study, and other available literature, statements similar in meaning have been grouped together.

Career Interests Vs. Personal Interests

Since the lives of the great majority of working women include responsibilities and interests outside their jobs, are women less interested or less devoted to their jobs than men? Must a married woman's job interest be subservient to that of her husband?

It should be remembered that the vast majority of male

executives were married, while most of the women were single or divorced. Besides, the respondents were generally in the over-forty age brackets and probably settled in their careers. Therefore it is not only natural but highly likely that there should be considerable difference of opinion between the sexes on certain issues and almost complete agreement on others. Although there was a substantial gap in percentage between male (52 percent) and female (69 percent) respondents, the majority rejected the idea that women were less interested in their jobs than men and more than three-fourths agreed that women with grownup children are as devoted to their careers as their male colleagues.

A highly significant aspect of the high proportion of male executives (76 percent) with favorable attitudes was brought to light in an examination of the interrelationships existing between attitude and work experience; those men who had supervised women, more importantly women in management, showed greater tendency to express positive attitudes toward women in business. This link between masculine attitude and working relationship of men and women was also found in the Harvard Business School study. "A strongly favorable attitude is expressed more often by men who have been superiors and peers of women managers than by those who have been subordinates to them."[9]

Other impartial studies point to the competence, devotion, and dependability of the older woman with respect to her job, as noted by one woman executive interviewed in the pilot study, "The married woman with a grown-up family is less likely to transfer from one company to another looking for greater opportunities."

A survey, conducted by Chicago's Social Research, Inc., of sixty women executives showed they "demonstrated greater day-to-day practicality, organizational skill, sensitivity to people and adaptability than men in comparable positions."[10] These findings appear to refute the

Figure 15
Dedication of Women to their Jobs

Women are less interested in their jobs than men.

As seen by MEN

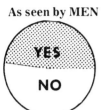

As seen by WOMEN

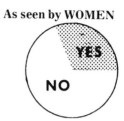

Married women's job interests must be subservient to those of their husbands.

As seen by MEN

As seen by WOMEN

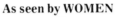

Women with grown-up children are as devoted to business careers as their male counterparts.

As seen by MEN

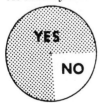

As seen by WOMEN

75

frequently expressed masculine opinion that women think first of their personal lives and give little priority to their business careers.

A very practical factor affecting a woman's promotability concerns her natural role as assistant or helper in the husband-wife relationship. Society deems woman subservient to man. Many companies and business executives alike feel it is not feasible to promote a married woman because her husband may be transferred. A large majority of our male respondents (69 percent) supported this view. However, the bare majority of women (51 percent) who agreed reflects the large proportion of unmarried women executives among our female respondents. Perhaps another inference could be that those women who were married had husbands established in their jobs and were not likely to seek other job opportunities. A look at responses from the undergraduate students showed even stronger support for the proposition that a woman's job interest must yield to that of her husband. The fact that two-thirds of the female students and over three-fourths of the male students were of this opinion seems to reflect the attitudes of parents.

Single women in business, particularly the young ones of marriageable age, are further handicapped simply because they are single. Whatever her intellectual capacity may be, the prime ambition of the average American woman is marriage and a family. Many girls think of a job as a short interlude between college and marriage. However, when we asked the responding companies to state their policies regarding promotion of single women, very few firms felt that the possibilities of leaving the firm due to marriage and family were drawbacks to promoting unmarried women. Yet the personal opinions of the respondent managers to a somewhat analogous statement verified the more common belief that women want families, not careers.

This concept of personal life versus business career for

women does not apply to all females. There are those who obtain satisfaction and fulfillment primarily through their work, the so-called career-oriented type, who are not interested in a home and family. If a single woman decides on a career rather than marriage is she as content in her job as a man? Definitely "yes" replied men (73 percent) and very decidedly "yes" said the women (85 percent). Male government officials (89 percent) were even more vigorous in their positive attitudes than most of the respondent female managers that the career-minded single woman functions successfully and happily in her chosen field.

Figure 16
Attitudes of Single Women Toward Business Careers

Single women anticipate marriage rather than a career.

As seen by MEN   As seen by WOMEN

Single women who have decided on a business career are as content in their jobs as men.

As seen by MEN   As seen by WOMEN

The results of students' opinions, however, suggest not only their inexperience, but also adolescent evaluations of woman's basic role in life. Large numbers of male students and a substantial proportion of the girls found it difficult to believe that any woman could judge a career to be more gratifying than motherhood.

	Male Students	Female Students
Single women who have decided on a business career are as content in their jobs as men.	49 %	55 %

Hazards in Promotion of Women

The rationale behind pessimistic attitudes toward women in management often includes the idea that women are poor risks for managerial training because they are in and out of the labor force more frequently than men. On the opposite side, statistics show that the rise in business expansion, the emergence of new enterprises and the ever-growing spread of government agencies have resulted in high mobility for men. The questionnaire cited three statements relating to the risks involved in considering women for potential management from the standpoint of mobility and asked the responding executives to give their views.

The majority of executives of both sexes agreed with the general statement that a man is a better investment for management training than a woman. But the significant point was the variation in responses. Male attitudes were almost universally in favor of men (89 percent were of this opinion), while a scant majority (53 percent) of females felt men had the advantage. A look at the returns by industry showed that men in government had less support from the argument (74 percent) than men in business (92 percent). A curious and unexpected observation was seen in responses from female executives in merchandising and banking firms, industries usually considered as offering greater opportunities for women, in that most female respondents (70 percent) favored men as being better investments for management development.

The specific issue, mobility of men versus women, received somewhat less vigorous response from men, but indicated an apparent disparity in women's thinking. The majority of females (56 percent) said, "yes," it is too much of a gamble to spend thousands of dollars in management training on women of child-bearing age. At the same time, the majority of women (59 percent) said the mobility of young males makes them just as risky. On the other hand, three out of four male respondents believed the possibility of pregnancy caused young women to be poor investments and two in every three felt that mobility of young men did not present as serious a problem to the company in potential loss of managers.

There are many examples of well-prepared young women who have been bypassed in favor of men for positions that lead into management training programs simply because young women are less likely than men to want a business career. The turnover rate for young women is greater than for men. Most women work for a while before marriage and a family, then place home responsibilities first until the children are grown. The write-in comment of one male executive seems to convey the view of many, "You don't think of a woman as being executive material until she has passed the child-bearing age. Then experience and education count."

Nonetheless, occupational mobility among young men today is considerably greater than in past years. Rèsumès showing a variety of experience are looked upon with favor, since knowledge gained from association with other businesses is considered an asset. On the one hand, many companies are pirating talent for key positions from competitive firms and, on the other hand, promising young

A man is a better investment for potential managerial training than a woman.

As seen by MEN

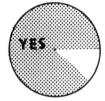

As seen by WOMEN

The promotion of any woman of child-bearing age is risky for a firm spending thousands of dollars in management training.

As seen by MEN

As seen by WOMEN

The mobility of young male executives makes an investment in male training as risky as that of females of child-bearing age.

As seen by MEN

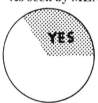

As seen by WOMEN

men are often impatient for promotion and find the quickest way to advance is by changing employers. This same vein of thinking was reported by a top woman executive of a large industrial manufacturing concern. She is quoted as saying, "Basically my work is people problems. As far as turnover is concerned, I haven't noticed much difference between the sexes except the reasons for leaving. If a woman likes what she does and feels she's doing something worthwhile, she'll stay. Some of the women who have worked for me leave and have babies, and then they come back." Another interesting excerpt from an article on this subject appeared in the London Times:

> Ford is one of the rare companies prepared to cut a swathe through the old cliche that women are a patently bad risk for management training schemes because of the marriage casualty risk—an attitude that overlooks that men are also liable to leave the firm that trained them. "Trainees pay off in two years," says Ford's personnel manager. "If women leave then to have babies, it's no different from our point of view to finance a man leaving for a higher salary." [12]

Certainly women's biological role is not going to change, but whether the marriage prejudice will continue to handicap young women may, to some degree, depend on changes in the mobility rate of males and possibly on attitude changes by women toward careers.

Women's Work Hours and the Law

Company attitudes, discussed previously, indicated that legislation limiting the number of hours women are permitted to work had little effect on their consideration for management positions. Our responding executives were of the same opinion. Although most states have stringent laws regulating the work patterns of certain categories of female employees, professional women and those whose salary or job classification places them in managerial positions are generally exempt. The image of an executive is not the nine to five worker and most women managers work the long hours of their male counterparts.

	Yes	
	Men	**Women**
Legislation limiting the time in-volvement of women reduces their usefulness as executives.	36 %	28 %

Women's Assets for Management

Do women possess special, unique characteristics to qualify them for executive positions? The respondent male and female managers were asked whether the special female abilities were utilized more effectively in staff positions or in supervisory posts.

The fact that a small percentage of both male and female executives were of the opinion that women were more apt to identify with the company than men may possibly be inferred as meaning that women in management were more faithful or devoted to the company than men. It may also suggest that women seek prestige and therefore are more inclined than men to identify their work with the company.

The majority of male managers (68 percent) felt that women function more effectively in staff rather than line assignments compared to approximately half of the women (52 percent). Woman managers tend to be in jobs where the "woman's point of view" is important, such as personnel work, supervisors of women, or in situations where they deal with women clients, or buy apparel for women customers. In comparing responses by type of business, there was considerable discrepancy between the female executives in merchandising firms and those in manufacturing companies. Almost twice as many of the women in manufacturing firms (79 percent) as those in merchandising (43 percent) felt women belong in staff positions, which is an indication of the high proportion of professional women respondents from the manufacturing industry. This may also reflect the attitude of those who advocate that women should not "buck the odds" against them in management, but instead, should seek professional positions.

Figure 18
Women's Special Abilities and Attributes

Women's specialized abilities are best captured through staff rather than line assignments.

As seen by MEN

As seen by WOMEN

Women in management positions identify more with the company than do men in management positions.

As seen by MEN

As seen by WOMEN

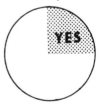

Male and female manager respondents in this survey support the contention that there are basic personality and attitude characteristics in women that mitigate against their promotion to higher managerial positions. Many of these characteristics are related to the biological and social role accorded women in our culture. But whatever the reasons underlying these female attitudes, the end result is the lack of acceptance of women in managerial ranks.

The next chapter prods more deeply into male and female attitudes to determine what deep-seated prejudices exist against women at work.

Notes

1. It is rather surprising that "Attention to Detail" received as much support as was evidenced, since this characteristic is generally associated with lower and middle levels of management.

2. The percentage of respondents who left this question blank was considerably greater than for any other part of the questionnaire, which would seem to imply that a substantial number of executives either perceived the characteristics to be applicable equally to both sexes, or were undecided. Therefore, the percentages shown in Figure 14 are based on the number of actual responses, and the difference between 100 percent and the percent given represents the proportion of respondents who considered the characteristic more common to men.

3. "What Makes Gertrude Run?" *The Management Review*, April 1960, p. 60.

4. G. W. Bowman et al, "Are Women Executives People?" *Harvard Business Review*, July August 1965, p. 28.

5. "How Good are Women Bosses?" *Changing Times*, April 1967, p. 16.

6. Marya Mannes, "Let's Face It: Women are Equal, But...," *McCall's*, September 1965, p. 159.

7. John B. Parrish and Jean S. Block, "The Future for Women in Science and Engineering," *Bulletin of the Atomic Scientists* (May, 1968), p. 47.

8. Betty Beale, "Johnson Champion of Women," *Los Angeles Times*, February 16, 1964, Section E, p. 6.

9. Bowman et al, op. cit., p. 166.

10. "Women at the Top," *Newsweek*, June 27, 1966, p. 76.

11. Marilyn Mercer, "Women at Work: Is There Room at the Top?" *The Saturday Evening Post*, July 27, 1968, p. 21.

12. Patricia Rowan, "Wooing Women into Industry," *London Times*, January 15, 1967.

7 Managerial Prejudices Toward Women in Management

The remaining issues about which the questionnaire sought opinions of responding executives could be classified as prejudice, discrimination, or deep-set preconvictions about women in management which are deeply entrenched in our culture. In the last sixty years women have campaigned vigorously and successfully for opportunities to prove their capabilities. Women have been particularly successful in government agencies, primarily because of equal opportunity laws and the fact that government has not always been attractive to aspiring male managers. But in business, except for merchandising and banking which have also not been as attractive to aspiring male managers as other industries, women have not fared well in reaching the managerial ranks.

We have examined company attitudes and experience in utilizing women as managers, and we have studied male and female attitudes toward women as managers. These conclusions support the position that women are considered not to have the appropriate characteristics or the attitudes toward work when compared with males. But is this effect rather than cause? Do the prejudices against women as managers run so deep in our society that women have come to accept them as truths?

The militant group of women proclaim there are no justifiable reasons for excluding females from positions of authority, that they are held back simply because of masculine prejudice. On the other hand, many businessmen say that women are not made managers because they do not make good managers. We attempted to further explore this controversial subject by examining the attitudes of the successful male and female executives responding to this survey. Attitudes of college students, who were queried on the same propositions, add emphasis to the executive study, from the standpoint of the upcoming generation of businessmen and businesswomen.

Logical and Emotional Attributes of Women

Almost three-fourths of the men (71 percent) and a significant percentage of women (49 percent) agreed that women are basically more emotional and less rational than men. Both male and female students demonstrated even greater support for the proposition. It can be assumed then that both generations of respondents believe that women's psychological makeup makes them unfit for work that requires objectivity, analytical skills, or careful reasoning. As reported earlier, the results of the Harvard study showed that half (51 percent) of the participating male executives felt women were temperamentally unsuited for management, which supports our findings.

Despite the fact that almost half (49 percent) of the women executives supported the view of the men, the majority, slim as it may be, protested that women were as emotionally stable and of equal intellectual ability with

Figure 19
Logical and Emotional Attributes of Women

Women are less logical and more emotional than men.

As seen by MEN

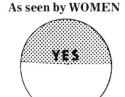

As seen by WOMEN

Male Students-YES-78%
Female Students-YES-55%

Women are more sensitive to the emotions of others and can better understand the all important human relations consideration in managing subordinates.

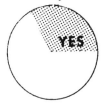

As seen by MEN

As seen by WOMEN

Male Students-YES-36%
Female Students-YES-51%

men. It is interesting to note that, with few exceptions, literature written by men agrees with the male point of view and that authored by women supports the women's outlook. Men say women cannot take the pressures required of an executive; they become tense under stress and let intuition take over instead of thinking the problem through to a logical conclusion. Women say this attitude is pure subterfuge and an attempt to camouflage male feelings of inferiority.

Perception and Empathy in Women

Another facet in the nature of people concerns their emotional sensitivity to others. Skill in human relations is a fundamental requisite for all managers. Numerous problems in business arise from misunderstandings between subordinates' needs and company goals. But the capacities of people to understand the needs and problems of others and to be instrumental in bringing about satisfactory solutions to the mutual benefit of employee and employer vary widely between individuals of both sexes. When we asked the respondents to state which sex was more likely to possess the quality "Perception and Empathy," the majority (80 percent) of the female executives believed this was a feminine characteristic and so did half (50 percent) of the male executives (see Figure 14).

In this portion of the questionnaire we attempted to pursue this thinking by suggesting that because of women's sensitivity to others they made better managers of subordinates than men do. The majority of male executives (67 percent) denied the statement. Conversely, almost the same percentage of female executives (63 percent) agreed that women do make better managers than men because of the female capacity to understand subjectively the feelings of subordinates. By comparison, a smaller percentage of female students (51 percent) had the same opinion as the female executives, which may imply that almost half of the girls had no ambition to become managers or, more importantly, had similar attitudes to those of the male students and executives. Apparently, a woman's ability to see another's point of view is not necessarily correlated with her ability to handle people.

Men and Women Do Not Like To Work for Women

We come now to the portion of the questionnaire designed specifically to evoke opinions of our male and female responding executives on issues dealing with preconceived ideas of women's place in life. Although many forces hinder women from being accepted into management, the predominant theme running through much of the literature on this subject centers in prejudice against women, based on certain deeply rooted convictions, namely: men, as well as women, do not like to work for women; and differences between the sexes cause problems in working relationships.

Results of the Harvard survey showed that the majority of both the male (82 percent) and the female (75 percent) respondents gave "Prejudice against women in work outside the home is very deeply rooted in our culture" as a reason for persisting negative attitudes.[1] In the same study, only a few of the men (9 percent) and women (15 percent) agreed to the statement, "Men feel comfortable working for women."[2]

Findings of our survey indicate very similar attitudes. The majority of both sexes (over 80 percent) supported the statement, "Men do not like to work for women," and that there is persisting prejudice against women in most industries. A highly significant point evidenced in our study and confirmed by the Harvard study is the correlation between attitude and proposition. The more specific the premise, the more favorable masculine attitudes appear to be. For example, the majority of the male respondents (82 percent) were of the opinion that men did not like to work for women, but only one-third (35 percent) said women were not accepted by subordinates on the basis of managerial talents and barely half (58 percent) perceived that subordinates of a woman executive experienced feelings of inferiority. The outlook of the women executives, on the other hand, was even more negative than that of the men. The vast majority (82 percent) believed that women managers did create problems of insecurity and inferiority among subordinates of both sexes.

Figure 20
Reasons For Prejudice

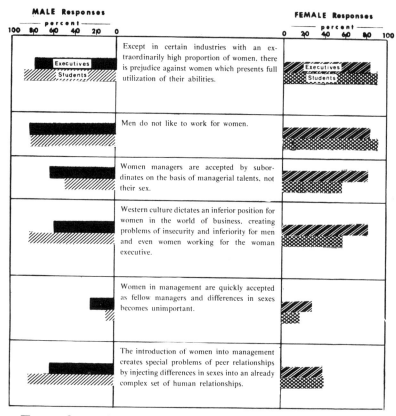

Examples of resistance to women managers by subordinates is found in other writings. A survey of 30,000 Federal service employees disclosed that the majority said men make better supervisors than women, and stated:

While many women do dislike serving under women, surveys show that **most** women do not care much one way or another. It's the men, though, who control business and industry and any woman trying to break into management ranks has to contend with masculine attitudes.[3]

Other articles noted this same problem for men working for women:

A young man who works for a distinguished woman lawyer spent a good deal of time declaring that no reasonable, intelligent man would have any objections to working for a really competent woman. "But, when my wife is a little bit sore at me she always introduces her to everybody saying, 'This is Geraldine. She's Robert's boss.' And that really gets to me."[4]

To most men, the prospect of working for a woman is flatly repellent. One recent survey showed that virtually all men interviewed who had never worked for a woman said they would refuse to take such a job. But half of those who had worked for women said they would do it again.[5]

The previous quotation agrees with observations found in this study as well as other surveys; namely, men who have had working experience with women as subordinates, peers, or supervisors are more likely to have favorable attitudes toward women managers.

As noted earlier, women have received acceptance into management fields in which "the woman's point of view" is considered important, such as personnel work, office management, department store merchandising, and social work. These areas employ a high proportion of female workers. The Bell Telephone System is an outstanding employer of large numbers of women. More than half of their employees are women, and "of the telephone company workers whose jobs pay a top salary of $10,000 or more, 10 percent are female—and this is an enormous jump over the national average."[6]

However, in industries where male workers predominate, is there prejudice against women which prevents full utilization of their talents? Large numbers of male and female respondents (78 percent of the men, 83 percent of the women) agreed there was prejudice. Many instances of discrimination are cited in literature; such as:

> I was in line for the job of director of public relations and everybody thought I'd get it, but the job went to some man out in left field. I was far better educated, had broader experience in the field and in handling staff and budgets, but the board of directors would never accept a woman.[7]

> I answered an ad for "management trainee, college graduate, sociology major," but the employment agency man said, "Sorry, the company doesn't want a broad."[8]

> Many of the men who preside over American business continue to cling relentlessly to the old shibboleth that a woman's place is with diapers, not debentures.[9]

One of the women executives interviewed in the pilot study supported this view: "Frankly, I prefer to work in a 'woman's profession,' rather than bucking constant prejudice."

Another aspect of our study, and one which will have significant impact on the future status of women in business concerns the attitudes of the students. A high degree of negativism prevailed in the attitudes of both male and female undergraduates. Note that the majority of the boys (84 percent, as compared to 58 percent of male executives) and over half of the girls (62 percent, as compared to 43 percent of female executives) agreed that subordinates of a woman felt insecure and inferior. This attitude may imply that young men resent the idea of women in management from the standpoint of their own expectations; that is, women may usurp managerial positions from the up-coming male generation.

Acceptance of Women in Management as Peers

Turning from attitudes toward women as managers to opinions of women managers as peers, we find a striking similarity of view between male and female respondents on one point and a wide difference of opinion on another. A decided minority of executives (26 percent of the men, 28 percent of the women) agreed with the statement, "Women in management are quickly accepted as fellow managers and differences in sexes become unimportant." Except for one industry, merchandising, reactions among respondents of the other industries did not vary to any significant extent. In merchandising, however, it is interesting to note the opposite points of view of the male and female respondents; almost half (41 percent) of the men said women in management were accepted on an equal basis as men in management, but not one woman supported this view. Perhaps these women had experienced the resentment of their male colleagues to even a greater degree than had three out of four women executives in other industries. The strong feminine opposition to members of their own sex might also suggest that some women disapprove of other women managers. This inference is supported in the Harvard study, where it was found that 17 percent of the female respondents were either "indifferent" or "unfavorable" to the idea of women in management and a third (34 percent) were only "mildly favorable."[10]

To explore further the attitudes of men and women toward the concept of women on the management team, respondents were asked to submit their views on the specific issue: "The introduction of women into management creates special problems of peer relationships by injecting differences in sexes into an already complex set of human relationships." Responses to this point indicated a wide discrepancy of opinion between the sexes. A substantial proportion of the male executives (63 percent) agreed that the presence of women added one more problem to the close personal associations required of members of management. The women executives, on the other hand, strongly rejected the idea, and response from the female students showed virtually identical consistency of opinion. Almost two-thirds of both groups believed that differences between the sexes created no problems at the management level. A highly significant point which supports these findings was evidenced in the atypical replies of the women executives in merchandising. Considering female response as a whole, only one-third (37 percent) agreed with the principle that mixing the sexes at the management level caused additional problems, but over two-thirds (71 percent) of the women in merchandising firms expressed this opinion.

It is possible that these women may not be representative of the entire group of women executives in merchandising, yet it seems reasonable that executives who are willing to participate in a study devoted strictly to the status of women would be more likely to have favorable attitudes toward women. The male executives in merchandising firms did show somewhat less resistance to women (56 percent) than the average male response (63 percent). This irregularity of pattern indicated by the female executives could very well imply situations peculiar to their own firms.

Attitudes of the male students, however, were in direct contrast to those of the girls. The fact that the majority (84 percent) of the young college men, compared to slightly over a third (39 percent) of the young women, were of the opinion that women, simply because of their sex, did not belong in management also indicates greater antipathy toward women than was demonstrated by the male businessmen (63 percent). This is another instance of the strong negative attitude of young males toward females in positions of authority, which reinforces the conclusions drawn from previous data and is further supported by other studies. Since older men tend to express less unfavorable attitudes than younger men, it seems logical to assume that young men fear competition by women may reduce their own opportunities.

A more optimistic outlook for women was expressed in a

statement made by the editor of an intercollegiate publication, **Moderator,** which "keeps a finger on the pulse of the male undergraduate,"

> Guys today don't have any particular feeling about working with women. They're used to them in classes, in organizations. Besides that, a lot of their mothers worked. The masculinity of a man today depends on other things. Keeping women in the home was their fathers' hang-up. [11.]

Our findings and that of other surveys do not support this more tolerant view toward women at work. The Harvard study found the same intolerance:

> Psychologists stress the young male's revolt against female domination in home and school, which may be another factor in the high correlation between youth and negative attitudes toward women managers among the male respondents. [12]

Our questionnaire was not designed to delve into the underlying causes of the problems created for men and women in management by virtue of difference in the sexes. However, a survey of other writings disclosed some interesting aspects which may well lie behind the attitudes of our responding executives. It is significant that the great majority of awkward situations mentioned in the literature involve female complaints of prejudicial treatment by men, rather than male rejection of women. The large number of top-ranking women reporting conflicts between the sexes appears correlated with the greater percentage of our responding female executives (compared to males) who reported problems.

One highly relevant factor concerns the very nature of femininity. To face the problems of being a woman in a man's world, many career women feel it necessary to lose some of their feminine qualities. As one woman president said, "When you get out into the business world you acquire the manner of an executive. When I deal with a man in business, I'm another man." [13] Likewise, the

95

consensus of the women participants in the training seminars for middle management at the University of Southern California was that "a woman had to defeminize herself with her male associates, yet not become mannish to the point other women distrust her and men feel uncomfortable."[14]

Some women attempt to disguise their sex by using their initials rather than first names. This method of deception has presented some embarrassing complications at times, as described by one female executive, "It got me on lots of lists for men only and I received lots of invitations to things like ski weekends for young male executives."[15]

Other women claim that women managers often encounter the dilemma of being excluded from dining at men's clubs. One such instance is reported of a woman bank official, who was invited to lunch at a Wall Street Men's Club, but had to ride to the dining room in the service elevator.[16] Another example is cited of a top-ranking woman executive who was asked to address a group of male executives, but who also encountered the humiliating experience of being required to take the freight elevator to the luncheon headquarters.[17]

Negative attitudes on the part of men appear confined to certain areas, principally those revolving around the tendency of women executives to demand equality, to try to be masculine, to insist on asserting their ego and to be domineering and aggressive.

An interesting point concerning masculine and feminine reactions was reported in the Harvard study in answer to the question, "Do men reveal a sense of their own insecurity when they object to women in general? Definitely yes, say women (79 percent). Yes, but barely, say men (51 percent)."[18] Other studies disclose similar feminine viewpoints. In the opinion of a woman sociologist (which may reflect the attitudes of many of our women respondents), masculine resistance to women falls into two categories:

The old kind was ideological—that is, men simply believed that women weren't as good as they were. Now there's a new kind of anti-feminism going on. It's defensive. They think women are as good as they are, and they fear the competition.[19]

There are businessmen and women who deny that prejudice exists, but they are definitely in the minority. Some say that the barriers against women are down and they support their argument by citing examples of successful women in the professions and in all levels of business management. But, as pointed out earlier, the fact that examples do exist merely emphasizes the minimal number of women executives.

The U.S. Labor Department has predicted that the female labor force by 1980 will reach about 32,000,000, more than half again as large as it was in 1960. Much of the rise is expected to be among married women.[20] Other writers point to the critical shortage of trained personnel in our affluent society. More and more young women are seeking higher educational levels than their mothers and, as the need for managerial talent increases, industry will be faced with the necessity to consider women as a management resource.

Times of shortage are times of opportunity, particularly for victims of prejudice. Most executives today agree that there is prejudice against women, that there are boundaries dividing men's work from women's work. Despite the fact that the executives responding to our survey were employed in firms where the proportion of women managers (6 percent) far exceeded the national average (2 percent), two of every three men were of the opinion that bringing males and females together in management situations creates special problems in peer relationships.

Those women who have succeeded in reaching their goals are usually women possessing exceptionally strong motivation and who have overcome the odds against them by virtue of sheer ability. The outlook of the college students, who represent the next generation of businessmen and women, does not seem to offer much encouragement to women.

More importantly, perhaps, than the attitudes of men are the attitudes of women themselves. Women play an important part in perpetuating the prejudices against themselves. Granted that opportunities for women do exist and will continue to increase, it is true that women's participation in the business world is largely a matter of choice. They can usually decide if, when, and how long they wish to work. Many women feel that the sacrifices they must make in their personal lives to advance in the ranks of management are not worth the effort. Therefore, whether the proportion of women in management will increase substantially in the near future depends to a large degree on women's individual values and their desire and willingness to qualify and dedicate themselves to work entailing much responsibility.

Notes

1. G. W. Bowman, et al., "Are Women Executives People?" *Harvard Business Review*, July August, 1965, p. 164.

2. Ibid., p. 166.

3. "How Good are Women Bosses?" *Changing Times*, April 1967, p. 16.

4. Marilyn Mercer, "Women at Work: Is There Room at the Top?" *The Saturday Evening Post*, July 27, 1968, p. 20.

5. "Executives: Prettiest Veep," *Newsweek*, February 7, 1966, p. 77.

6. Mercer, op. cit., p. 20.

7. Ibid., p. 18.

8. Ibid., p. 17.

9. "Executives: Prettiest Veep," p. 76.

10. Bowman et al, op cit., p. 26.

11. Mercer, op. cit., p. 60.

12. Bowman et al, op. cit., p. 166.

13. "Executives: Prettiest Veep," p. 77.

14. Dorothy Townsend, "Executive Women: They're Right at 'Home' in the Office," *Los Angeles Times*, September 1, 1963, Section E, p. 2.

15. "Executives: Prettiest Veep," p. 77.

16. Mercer, op. cit., p. 18.

17. "Executives: Prettiest Veep," p. 77.

18. Bowman et al, op. cit., p. 28.

19. Mercer, op. cit., p. 20—quotes sociologist Helen M. Hacker.

20. Vera C. Perella, "Women and the Labor Force," *Monthly Labor Review*, February 1968, p. 12.

8   The Woman's Place in Management: A Redefinition

In today's world of turmoil and change, women have gradually awakened to the fact that they are treated like any other minority group—with discrimination, inadequate economic opportunity, and deeply rooted prejudice. The recent actions of the women's liberation movement and the congressional action to end any and all legal discrimination against women attest to the fact that women are demanding equal rights in all phases of modern life's activities. But this still leaves one basic question left unanswered: will women really exercise all these new-found rights? The evidence presented in this research study indicates that they will not.

Social and cultural values change slowly, even in the late 20th century. And there seem no alternatives, even in the future, which will eliminate the physiological differences between men and women which go a long way to defining the respective roles of men and women. In western society, the family is still sacred and our culture has defined women's role specifically as a wife and mother.

Are we on the threshold of redefining that role to allow the wife's career to have equal weight with that of the husband? As long as our social values place a higher value on the husband's career, business will continue to discriminate against women for managerial and professional positions.

Within these constraints, what can be done to enhance the role of women in management? What role should women play and how should they approach that role?

Scarce Resources

In the past, women have not competed with men intellectually. There would seem to be no reason why women who are equal to men in intelligence and business experience should not hold equal managerial positions. A study of the progress of children in elementary schools would even indicate that girls have a learning advantage over boys because of deeper interest and maturity. Let us then be rid of the myth that women are in any way not intellectually equal to men.

The common market countries of Europe (and even the United States to a lesser degree) have major labor shortages which can only be solved by importing workers from Spain, Greece, Yugoslavia, and Turkey. There is a chronic shortage of professional personnel, such as medical doctors, all over the world. Women are entering the labor market to a greater degree than at any other time in history, except for wartime periods. In many ways, the only major untapped human resource is women. But the argument has been advanced that, since women are basically only interested in marriage and having a family, they must be used for the more menial jobs and certainly rarely for management. Companies are unwilling to spend money training a woman who may leave the company shortly to fulfill family obligations. Often she is only earning a second income to supplement that of her husband on a temporary basis.

Unfortunately, these arguments are in the main true since there is overwhelming evidence to support them. But this eventual non-business role for women is carried over into the definition of what education and training the young woman is to receive. Certain professions and jobs have been reserved by tradition for women, and rarely do women step outside such traditional training in the schools and universities. It is almost an insidious plot, in which women as mothers often play the major part, which discourages young women from seeking the training and education which would qualify them for those jobs and positions normally reserved for men. A major criticism is made of women that they do not possess the qualifications for management and therefore they cannot be promoted to the managerial ranks. But our social values and traditions have predefined the woman's role so she does not seek to obtain the qualifications necessary to be considered for a managerial position.

We are in times of drastically changing social and cultural values but, like other groups against whom prejudice exists, there is a time lag before qualifications can meet aspiration levels for women. It is not enough to eliminate all legal discrimination since managerial and professional jobs only will be given to those qualified to fill them. The change must come first in education of women and this means a major campaign to encourage women to complete the education required for tomorrow's managers and professionals. The Master of Business Administration is fast becoming a prerequisite to obtaining managerial jobs but the number of women taking graduate training in our business schools is minuscule. Very little formal discouragement or such things as quota systems for the proportion of women admitted to graduate training in business exist today. This cannot be said for some other professions, but undoubtedly any such barriers will fall shortly to more militant women's groups.

We need more educated and trained women to supplement our already badly strained resources. But untrained women cannot and will not contribute anything like what is needed in the decade ahead.

A New Era—Managerial Mobility

A major finding of this research study was that discrimination exists against women for management because of the lack of mobility. Women are tied to particular locations and often particular hours of work because of family duties and responsibilities. But today a major necessity for managerial promotion is mobility to move from one part of the country to another or even overseas. Can a woman's marriage survive a preeminence of the wife's career over that of the husband? Will women who desire success in the business world have to give up marriage or alternatively marry men of such lesser stature so that the husband will give up his job to move to a new location to further his wife's career? This is a major difficulty which may force women to accept lesser positions than those for which they are qualified. Under present cultural conditions the male ego is easily bruised and there is some doubt whether most men could set aside their own careers. However, this assumes that the current mores and customs will continue which may not be the case. The trend toward unisex in clothes among certain segments of the younger generation may also carry over into careers. But the findings of this research study conclude that college students currently share the same prejudices or attitudes as their parents toward the place of women in management. And this is true for both men and women.

But there is one other major shift that has not been sufficiently well recognized by management in promoting men to managerial positions rather than women. There is the feeling that women have insufficient mobility to change locations but also have insufficient tenure of time with one company to justify the expense of a training program or on-the-job managerial experience. But the attrition rate among men in training is fantastically great. Banks, for example, find that some 50 percent of their management trainees terminate in the first year of a training program. In higher managerial positions it is uncommon to find a man who has not held at least two or three jobs with different companies. A case could be made that women have a higher degree of loyalty and might be less likely to leave a company for a better job elsewhere, but there is inadequate evidence to support this conclusion.

The present attitude is strong that women's inclination to place their jobs second to their families and to the careers of their husbands precludes them from serious consideration for management training if the company has a choice between training men or women. It will take many years of actual experience of women remaining in and contributing to managerial positions in business to change this deeply rooted attitude.

Redefinition of Women's Role Under the Law

There seems little doubt that the permissive culture of the 1970's will see a redefinition of the role of women under the law. Israel is living proof of such a redefinition, even conscripting young women for the army. And we will soon reach the stage where the young go-go air stewardess of the 1970's will be in her fifties and still flying. An interesting byproduct of this new equality under the law will be a demand by men that commercial airlines hire as many men as women as stewards, and that women pay alimony to men.

There may be losses for women as well as gains if there is complete equality under the law. One unsatisfactory byproduct of minimum wage laws is often the elimination of the substandard worker who cannot be sufficiently productive to justify the higher wage. The final result of high minimum wages may well be an increase in the number of welfare recipients. In the case of women, the problem may be that equality of wage levels will result in the replacement of some women by men in particular jobs. This may be especially true in the managerial ranks where companies will demand higher qualifications than may currently be possessed by women if the managerial salaries are to be equal for men and women. In the long run, this will result in women attaining higher qualifications to compete with the men, but it may have unsatisfactory results in the short run.

Certainly the clarification of the laws to permit women managers to work the same hours as their male counterparts should go a long way to removing a past complaint about women managers. The 40-hour week for managers seems to be a myth, with managers often working late or on weekends on company business. The use of management conferences is greatly on the increase and women will now be able to attend such conferences equally with their male counterparts. Of course, perhaps we have reckoned without the manager's wife who may object to her husband being away on a weekend conference with his attractive female boss.

Will the United States follow the Russian pattern of increasing equality of men and women, and if so, what are the consequences for the nation and for women? Are women willing to make the sacrifices inherent in sustaining such equal status—of stressing work as their main activity over marriage and the family? Or will there be major cultural and social changes which will permit women true freedom of action and complete equality? Certainly, as far as the law is concerned, there is no doubt that legal discrimination in any form will be outlawed, and that complete choice will be permitted the individual woman to choose her life and her career. But, just as racial discrimination is legally ended but still socially practiced, so may women find that this new-found legal equality is but a hollow shell in terms of social acceptance of woman's new role.

A Changing Culture—Women as Equals

Our research with college students would not support the thesis that the new permissive society will end discrimination against women in management. Birth control pills, abortions, and even a family without a husband as practiced in Sweden will undoubtedly become ever more readily acceptable socially. But will men readily accept women as their bosses, or will both men and women consider that the female is sufficiently rational and unemotional to be considered equally with men for top managerial positions? Again our research would deny that the attitudes of men and women have reached the stage where such promotions of women will become commonplace.

Yet the future holds great promise for greater equality for women. The labor shortage is going to force the hiring of a larger proportion of women in the future. Permissiveness in sexual mores, clothes, and life style must be extended to permit women greater freedom and eventual acceptance in whatever role they desire. Perhaps the most difficult question lies with women themselves—will they wish to exercise this freedom when they receive it? Stress patterns in management will undoubtedly not decrease, educational requirements will become more exacting, and work patterns of managers will become more intense. If women have the choice, will they decide to enter into this managerial jungle? Undoubtedly, only time will tell, and since change is so much a way of life in the 1970's, women may have this choice sooner than they expect.

How much will men resist this changing culture to permit women to be equals? Certainly the older generation of men will resist according women total equality because of their adherence to past traditions. Men and women in past generations have defined the role of women to be wives and mothers. Every change in this role has been resisted by men, from women's suffrage to working outside the homes. It is difficult to know why men have resisted granting greater rights to women. Perhaps the biological differences have led to psychological problems for the male—a need to emphasize his manhood by dominance over the female. Or perhaps such resistance has had its base in economic competition for jobs and wages. It is still a common argument that a woman should receive less pay than a man since the latter must support a family. But today the case is common where many families have two wage earners—the wife and the husband. Here the argument is advanced that the wife is only temporarily in the labor market to accumulate the necessary monies for a house or household goods, and that the man is still considered the principal wage earner.

There will be resistance to full equality for women, particularly in the promotion to higher managerial jobs. Such resistance will only lessen as women prove to men and to themselves that they have the qualifications and the abilities to produce equal or better results than men. Most successful women executives have noted that they have to have abilities far superior to those of their male counterparts, and that they have to play a game of remaining sufficiently feminine in order not to be rejected by men on a social-personal relations basis.

Motivation and Desire—The Critical Elements

It would seem that the time has come for women to gain full equality with men—but will they put forth the effort to grasp it? Some of the attributes found necessary for success in management, such as aggressiveness, have been found by women in their social role to repel men. Are women willing to risk alienating men, as well as other women, to cultivate such a managerial attribute as aggressiveness? If we consider that marriage is the normal state for both mature men and women, can a woman place as much emphasis on her career as her male counterpart and have her marriage survive?

Can there be a differentiation between the attributes required for the female manager and for the male manager which would permit equal opportunity for women? If men cannot accept harshness or aggressiveness in women, can women perform a managerial function utilizing more womenly attributes and be accepted? This is a critical point since it means accepting women as women rather than accepting women as managers per se. In other words, there would be two acceptable ways to perform a managerial job—one way for men and another for women—but there would be no preference for one way or the other. Current findings of the behavioral sciences in leadership would support the thesis that there is no one way to be successful as a manager, and that the old traitist definition of attributes required for leadership (attributes such as aggressiveness, decisiveness, etc.), is no longer accepted. This would support the possibility that women could determine their leadership patterns to suit their own personalities and strengths and not have to compete with men on the basis of male strengths.

If women could approach the performance of managerial tasks on this basis, many of the male criticisms of women as managers might be countered. Women would then be judged as men are judged—on the basis of results and not on personality attributes. But this still does not answer the criticism that women do not have the motivation or desire to be managers, except for a very few highly motivated and highly qualified women who have reached the top in the managerial ranks. Apparently, at the present time, women in general do not have such drive or motivation. The question is whether they will change in the coming years. The rise of militant women's organizations to demand greater rights for women has not been supported by overt action on the part of the majority of women. We do not see a major move by women to seek higher education for positions in management. It would seem possible to conclude that, certainly in the early 1970's, we do not expect that women will have the necessary drive or motivation to gain the qualifications necessary for higher managerial positions.

A Prescription for Action

This research study, and others quoted here, all point to the existence of prejudice against women in management. Some of the prejudices are related to the psychological makeup of women as compared to that of men, and these prejudices are held almost equally by men and women. It would seem that the remedy for such prejudices is for women to change their psychological makeup. But this seems to fly in the face of reality and at most can only be applied to children born in the past few years. The Communist countries have attempted to remove children from the family influence with some degree of success but such a move would not be in accord with our concepts of freedom of the individual. Can we expect today's mothers to raise their daughters in cultural patterns so totally different from their own traditions? The answer seems to be no, since we reject any change such as the hippie culture, which has attempted to raise children to have mores and customs different from those we normally accept.

The best prescription is for greater encouragement by parents for their daughters to receive equal education with their sons, and not just in the so-called women's professions. This encouragement should also recognize the fragile qualities of marriage and encourage young women to seek job experiences which will permit them to attain managerial positions and not to seek early marriage. The divorce rate is high and there seems to be no indication that it will decline in the years ahead. Women may find that they are not able to be fulfilled in marriage sufficiently and that they must seek the challenge of work and a management career. This is not to deprecate marriage as an institution or to consider that many if not the majority of women may still prefer the traditional marriage to maintaining a career with or without marriage.

Finally, women must seek to compete with men on their own terms rather than to try to adopt what our culture regards as "masculine" characteristics. Why shouldn't women be feminine and even seductive if that permits them to achieve success in a managerial career? This is not to advocate immorality of any sort but rather to encourage women to use all their female charms and powers and be women while being managers.

Appendix

Questionnaire on Women in Management for Male and Female Executives

QUESTIONNAIRE

UNIVERSITY OF SOUTHERN CALIFORNIA
GRADUATE SCHOOL OF BUSINESS ADMINISTRATION
OFFICE OF RESEARCH INSTITUTE FOR
BUSINESS AND ECONOMICS
UNIVERSITY PARK
LOS ANGELES. CALIFORNIA 90007

1 May 1965

CODE

INSTRUCTIONS

We are conducting a survey of management attitudes under a grant from the Business and Professional Women's Foundation. Our questionnaire has been designed to incur the minimum amount of time involvement to permit maximum return.
Please check all appropriate squares.   Section I is to be completed by the Personnel Department for **both** questionnaires.   The respondent is to complete Sections II, III and IV.

May we ask for your cooperation in completing the questionnaire, even if you do not utilize any women in management
positions in your organization? The BLUE questionnaire is to be completed by the President or other top management
executive with major decision responsibilities.   The PINK questionnaire is to be completed by the highest ranking
female executive.   If you have no female executives, then please return the PINK questionnaire with the notation
that there are no female executives.

May we take this opportunity to thank you for completing the questionnaire. It is through the cooperation of organizations such as yours that the University is able to make some contribution to a better understanding of management.

1

2

SECTION 1- COMPANY INFORMATION

SIZE OF COMPANY OR INSTITUTION (Number of Employees)

To 500	501-1000	1001-5000	5001-20,000	20,000-50,000	Over 50,000

3

TYPE OF BUSINESS

Manufacturing	Merchandising	Banking	Insurance	Transportation	Utilities	Government	Other

4

STATE IN WHICH RESPONDENT IS LOCATED _____

5

APPROXIMATE NUMBER OF MANAGEMENT POSITIONS
(Defined as at least one level above forelady or supervisor of direct labor personnel)

None	0-1%	1-2%	3-5%	6-10%	11-20%	21-50%	Over 50%

TYPES OF MANAGEMENT POSITIONS HELD BY WOMEN IN YOUR COMPANY

	Majority	Some	Few	None
Office Supervision				
Production, Merchandising, or Sales Supervision				
Staff Specialists or Professionals				
Policy and Major Decision-Making Responsibilities				

6

7

8

9

Does your firm normally fail to promote women to managerial positions because they are likely to marry, have
children, and therefore leave the firm?   YES ☐ NO ☐

10

Does the current legislation for a restricted work pattern (e.g., 40 hours per week) restrain your firm from
promoting women to management positions?   YES ☐ NO ☐

11

When a woman has returned to the labor market after raising a family, and has equivalent qualifications to male
applicants, would your firm normally consider her as a potential manager?

IF YES ☐ , WHICH OF THE FOLLOWING REASONS APPLY?

12

☐ Women managers are paid less than equivalent male managers

☐ There is a shortage of qualified male managers

☐ Men do not compete with women for jobs in our industry

☐ Women provide greater stability in remaining with the firm

115

☐ Women bring a woman's point of view into the firm

☐ Government regulations demand a non-discrimination ruling

☐ Other (Please specify) _____

IF NO ☐ , WHICH OF THE FOLLOWING REASONS APPLY?   13

☐ Too old to consider training

☐ Women do not make good managers in our company

☐ Most women do not have adequate business experience

☐ Women are unable to move from one geographic location

☐ Most women do not have adequate educational backgrounds

☐ Women lack drive and motivation for management

☐ Other (Please specify) _____

SECTION 11- RESPONDENT'S BACKGROUND

———— **Please Return Questionnaire in Return Envelope Enclosed** ————

14 MARITAL STATUS	15 AGE	16 EDUCATION	Yes	No	17 FAMILY BACKGROUND		
						Father	Mother	Husband or Wife
Single	20-29	High School Diploma			Non-supervisory job			
Married	30-39	College Degree			Management position			
Divorced	40-49	Graduate Degree			Professional job			
	50-59				Attended college			
	60-							

RESPONDENT START HERE

EXPERIENCE   18

Number of Years in Management Positions

Supervised Women in Non-Management Positions   YES ☐   NO ☐

Supervised Women in Management Positions   YES ☐   NO ☐

_____

PRESENT JOB TITLE _____

SECTION 111 -THE MANAGEMENT TASK

Which of the following characteristics, skills, or tasks would you consider as important and necessary for 1st line supervision, middle management, and top management?

CHARACTERISTIC	1st LINE SUPERVISION			MIDDLE MANAGEMENT			TOP MANAGEMENT			
	Little or no	Some	Great deal	Little or no	Some	Great deal	Little or no	Some	Great deal	
Planning within Budgets										
Setting Objectives										19
Selecting Personnel										20
Results Oriented										21
People Oriented										22
Handles Detail										23
Delegates										24
Supervises										25
Controls People										26
Controls Things										27
Develops People										28
Self Regulating										29
										30

Individualists										31
Report Writing Ability										32
Works Under Pressure										33
Oral Communication Ability										34
Conference Leadership Ability										35
Team Work Ability										36
Good Appearance and Demeanor										37
Must be Able to Compromise										38
Ability to Take Risks										39
Desires Peer Group Recognition										40
Needs to Conform										41

SECTION 1V- SURVEY OF ATTITUDES

Certain characteristics and qualifications can be considered as (1) important or unimportant for upper levels of management, and (2) to be more common to or more often found in men than women.   Please give your opinion by checking the appropriate squares.

CHARACTERISTIC	REQUIREMENT FOR UPPER MANAGEMENT		MORE LIKELY TO BE FOUND IN		
	Yes	No	Males	Females	
Perception and Empathy					42
Emotional Stability					43
Consistency & Objectivity					44
Analytical Ability					45
Attention to Detail					46
Decisiveness					47
Creativity					48
Loyalty					49
Interest in People					50

PLEASE NOTE YOUR **PERSONAL** OPINION IN ANSWERING THE FOLLOWING QUESTIONS

	Yes	No	
Women are less interested in their jobs than men			51
Women in management are quickly accepted as fellow managers and difference in sexes becomes unimportant			52
Single women anticipate marriage rather than a career			53
Married women's job interests must be subservient to those of their husbands			54
Women in management positions identify more with the company than do men in management positions			55
Women can bring specialized abilities and perceptions, such as the woman's point of view into a business, but these abilities are best captured through staff rather than line assignments			56
Except in certain industries with an extraordinarily high proportion of women, there is prejudice against women in management which prevents full utilization of their talents and abilities			57
Men do not like to work for women			58
Single women who have decided on a business career are as content in their jobs as men			59
A man is a better investment for potential managerial training than a woman			60
Women managers are accepted by subordinates on the basis of managerial talents, not their sex			61
Western culture dictates an inferior position for women in the world of business, creating problems of insecurity and inferiority for men and even women working for the woman executive			62
Women are less logical and more emotional than men			63
The promotion of any woman of childbearing age is risky for a firm spending thousands of dollars in management training			64
Women are more sensitive than men to the emotions of others and therefore can better understand the all important human relations consideration in managing subordinates			65
The mobility of young male executives makes an investment in male training as risky as that in females of childbearing age			66
The introduction of women into management creates special problems of peer relationships by injecting differences in sexes into an already complex set of human relationships			67
Current legislation limiting the time involvement of women reduces their usefulness as executives			68
Women with grown-up children are as devoted to business careers as their male counterparts			69

Bibliography

Books and Reports

Cassara, Beverly Benner (Ed.). *American Women: The Changing Image.* Boston: Beacon Press, 1962.

Ellman, Edgar S. *Managing Women in Business.* Waterford: Prentice-Hall, 1963.

Friedan, Betty. *The Feminine Mystique.* New York: N. W. Harton & Co., 1963.

Report of the President's Commission on the Status of Women, *American Women.* Washington, D.C. U.S. Government Printing Office, 1963.

Roesch, Roberta. *Women in Action—Their Questions and Answers.* New York: The John Day Co., 1967.

Articles and Speeches

"The Battle of the Sexes is Over. Who Won? We Did," *Ladies' Home Journal,* February 1967, pp. 66 and 136.

Beale, Betty."Johnson Champion of Women," *Los Angeles Times,* February 16, 1964, Section E, p. 6.

Block, Jean Libman. "Who Says American Women are 'Trapped'?" *Los Angeles Times,* This Week Magazine, Oct. 6, 1963, pp. 10-11 and 14-15.

Boltz, Mrs. Sue. "A Lady Shows Them How It's Done," *Business Week,* October 15, 1966, pp. 134-138 and 142, 144.

Bowman, G. W., N. B. Worthy and S. A. Greyser. "Are Women Executives People?" *Harvard Business Review,* July/August 1965, pp. 14-28 and 164-178.

Chipps, G. and C. Jessup. "Leave it to the Supergirls," *Look,* June 25, 1968, pp. m12-15.

Cohen, Wilbur J. "Seminar on Manpower Policy and Program: Manpower Policies for the 1970's," *U. S. Report 1967.*

Cousins, Margaret. "Why Women Don't Succeed," *Los Angeles Times,* This Week Magazine, February 9, 1964, pp. 10 and 19.

"Draft Declaration on Elimination of Discrimination Against Women," *U.N. Monthly Chronicle,* November 1967, pp. 37-39.

"Executives: Prettiest Veep," *Newsweek,* February 7, 1966, p. 69.

Feiffer, J. "Men Really Don't Like Women," *Look,* January 11, 1966, p. 60.

Fleming, Thomas J. "The World of Women at Work," *Los Angeles Times,* This Week Magazine, February 9, 1964, pp. 2, 4, 6-7.

"From the Women: What About Our Job Rights?" *U. S. News & World Report,* July 4, 1966, pp. 61-62.

Goldberg, P. "Are Women Prejudiced Against Women?" *Trans-Action,* April 1968, pp. 28-30.

Guyer, Donna Dickey. "Brass Hats in Petticoats," *National Business Woman,* July 1958.

"How Good Are Women Bosses?" *Changing Times,* April 1967, pp. 15-17.

Johnson, Lynda Byrd. "The Working Girl, 1967," *McCall's,* May 1967, pp. 78-79 and 159-162.

Johnstone, E. "Women in Economic Life," *Annals of the American Academy,* January 1968, pp. 102-114.

Klein, David. "How Much of a Man's World Is It?" *Seventeen,* November 1967, pp. 210, 214, 216.

"The Labor Month in Review. Sex and Equal Opportunity Rights," *Monthly Labor Review,* August 1967, pp. III-IV.

Luce, Clare Booth. "Is it NOW or Never for Women?" *McCall's,* April 1967, pp. 48-50.

Macy, John W. Jr. "Unless We Begin Now," *Vital Speeches of the Day,* September 1, 1966, pp. 678-682.

Mannes, Marya. "Let's Face It: Women Are Equal, But . . . ," *McCall's,* September 1965, pp. 18 and 159.

McCormack, Patricia. "Career Girls Up Against 10 Obstacles," *Los Angeles Times,* October 6, 1963, Section E, p. 9.

McCormack, Thelma. "Styles in Educated Females," *Nation,* January 23, 1967, pp. 117-118. (Review of *Life Styles of Educated Women* by Eli Ginsberg and others.)

Mercer, Marilyn. "Women at Work: Is There Room at the

Top?" *The Saturday Evening Post,* July 27, 1968, pp. 17-21 and 60.

Morse, Muriel. "The Ever Widening Horizon of Management," Speech, University of Southern California Seminar, 1963.

"Official Word on Job Rights for Women: Official Guidance by EEOC," *U.S. News & World Report,* November 22, 1965, pp. 90-91.

Parrish, John B. and Jean S. Block. "The Future for Women in Science and Engineering," *Bulletin of the Atomic Scientists,* May 1968, pp. 46-49.

Perham, P. "Women, Industry's Newest Challenge," *Dun's Review,* August 1966, pp. 36-37.

Perella, Vera C. "Women and the Labor Force," *Monthly Labor Review,* February 1968, pp. 1-19.

"Petticoats Rustle on the Executive Ladder," *Business Week,* September 29, 1962, pp. 50-51.

Reeves, Nancy. "Better Half," *Nation,* November 7, 1966, pp. 490-492. (Review of *The Better Half,* by Andrew Sinclair.)

Rosenfeld, C. and Vera C. Perella. "Why Women Start and Stop Working: A Study in Mobility," *Monthly Labor Review,* September 1965, pp. 1077-1082.

Rowan, Patricia. "Wooing Women into Industry," *London Times,* January 15, 1967.

Ryscavage, Paul M. "Changes in Occupational Employment Over the Past Decade," *Monthly Labor Review,* August 1967, pp. 27-30.

Tebbel, John. "People and Jobs," *Saturday Review,* December 30, 1967, pp. 8-12 and 42.

Tillett, G. A. "Elimination of Discrimination Against Women: Report on 19th Session of the U.N. Commission on the Status of Women," *Department of State Bulletin 55,* August 22, 1966, pp. 284-288.

Townsend, Dorothy. "Executive Women: They're Right at 'Home' in the Office," *Los Angeles Times,* September 1, 1963, Section E, p. 2.

Turpin, Dick. "Women Bypassed in High Teaching Levels," *Los Angeles Times,* March 7, 1965, Section F, p. 1.

Wells, J. A. "Women College Graduates 7 Years Later," *Monthly Labor Review,* July 1967, pp. 28-32.

"What Makes Gertrude Run?" *The Management Review,* April 1960, pp. 59-60.

"Women at Beck and Call," *Forbes,* July 15, 1967, pp. 42-45.

"Women at the Top," *Newsweek,* June 27, 1966, pp. 76-78.